Solutions

Upper-Intermediate Workbook

Tim Falla, Paul A Davies

Wherever you see this symbol, you will find interactive practice in the corresponding section of the MultiROM.

IN YOUR CD PLAYER

Track
1 1F Speaking: Talking about photos, page 9
2 1F Speaking: Talking about photos, page 9
3 2F Speaking: Discussing pros and cons, page 17
4 Get ready for your exam 1, page 20
5 3F Speaking: Presenting arguments, page 27
6 3F Speaking: Presenting arguments, page 27
7 4F Speaking: Topic presentation, page 35
8 Get ready for your exam 2, page 38
9 5F Speaking: Talking about statistics, page 45

10 5F Speaking: Talking about statistics, page 45
11 6F Speaking: Expressing opinions, page 53
12 Get ready for your exam 3, page 56
13 7F Speaking: Role-play, page 63
14 8F Speaking: Discussion, page 71
15 Get ready for your exam 4, page 74
16 9F Speaking: Job interview, page 81
17 10F Speaking: Presentation, page 89
18 Get ready for your exam 5, page 92

1 Against the odds

A VOCABULARY
Talking about people

I can describe someone's personality.

1 Write the opposites of these personality adjectives.

1. **u n r** **d e p e n d a b l e** **r l i a b l e**

2. **s o p h i s t i c a t e d**

3. **i l l - m a n n e r e d**

4. **b i g - h e a d e d**

5. **c o n s i d e r a t e**

6. **c h e e r f u l**

2 Complete the sentences with the words in the box.

| broad-minded considerate modest grumpy naive self-confident |

1 My neighbours are so noisy at night. I wish they'd be more _____!

2 I can say anything I like in front of my grandmother. She's very _____ for her age.

3 It was very _____ of you to leave your bike unlocked and think nobody would steal it.

4 His exam results are always fantastic, but he's too _____ to talk about them.

5 My sister is so _____ – she's quite happy to sing in front of a room full of people.

6 Luke is so _____ – he's always in a bad mood.

●●●●● **Extension:** Comparisons with *as ...as*

3 Choose the correct word to complete the sentences.

1 The children had been as good as **ABC** / **gold** all morning.

2 Finally, after 10 years in prison, Rodney found himself as free as a **bird** / **bee**.

3 Stories about strange creatures who live deep in the forest are as old as **silk** / **the hills**.

4 You have to be as quiet as **an eel** / **a mouse**, or you'll wake my parents up.

5 Our dog looks quite fierce, but in fact, he's as gentle as a **lamb** / **mule**.

6 You should eat more. You're as thin as a **rake** / **feather**!

7 Julie has been as busy as a **bee** / **bird** getting everything ready for the conference.

8 Don't let Ben trick you into doing all his work – he's as sly as **an eel** / **a fox**!

●●●●●●● **CHALLENGE!** ●●●●●●●

Complete these sentences with your own ideas so that they show the meaning of the adjectives.

Grace is so argumentative. Last night, for example, she started an argument with a complete stranger in a café.

1 Martin is very considerate. He often _____

2 I wish you weren't so narrow-minded. You never _____

3 My mum is a very generous person. She always _____

4 Ruth is so unreliable. She never _____

Past and perfect tenses

1 Complete the sentences with the past simple or present perfect simple.

1 You can't be hungry. You _____ (eat) a bowl of pasta ten minutes ago!

2 Lauren is probably the most intelligent person I _____ (meet).

3 We _____ (catch) four fish already, and we've only been here an hour!

4 When he was a child, his family _____ (live) in India.

5 Don't put the laptop away – I _____ (not finish) using it yet.

6 I _____ (know) her for years, and I think she's very level-headed.

7 Gail picked up her coat and _____ (walk) out of the restaurant.

8 How many times _____ (you / phone) your boyfriend so far today?

2 Choose the best tense, simple or continuous, to complete the e-mails.

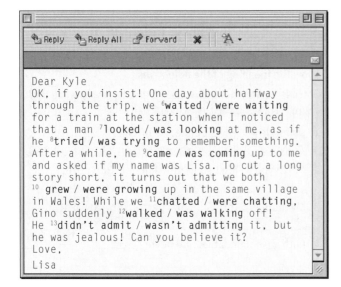

Dear Kyle
I'm sorry I haven't ¹**written / been writing** to you for so long. I've ²**meant / been meaning** to send you an e-mail ever since I ³**got / was getting** back to Peru from my trip around Chile and Argentina with my boyfriend, Gino. The trip was great, but unfortunately Gino and I ⁴**fell / was falling** out. I won't go into details. Anyway, we've only ⁵**seen / been seeing** each other once since then.
Love,
Lisa

Dear Kyle
OK, if you insist! One day about halfway through the trip, we ⁶**waited / were waiting** for a train at the station when I noticed that a man ⁷**looked / was looking** at me, as if he ⁸**tried / was trying** to remember something. After a while, he ⁹**came / was coming** up to me and asked if my name was Lisa. To cut a long story short, it turns out that we both ¹⁰**grew / were growing** up in the same village in Wales! While we ¹¹**chatted / were chatting**, Gino suddenly ¹²**walked / was walking** off! He ¹³**didn't admit / wasn't admitting** it, but he was jealous! Can you believe it?
Love,
Lisa

3 Complete each sentence with the past simple and past continuous.

1 It _____ (get) dark by the time we _____ (arrive) at the holiday chalet.

2 As I _____ (prepare) lunch, I _____ (cut) my hand.

3 They _____ (discover) some ancient ruins when they _____ (build) the new supermarket.

4 You _____ (start) talking while I _____ (talk)!

5 We _____ (just / leave) when the policeman _____ (knock) on the door.

6 When they _____ (find) Lewis, he _____ (live) in New York under a false name.

4 Complete the dialogue with an appropriate past tense of the verbs in brackets.

Kyle I saw Lisa last week. She ¹_____ (just /arrived) back from a year in Latin America.

Alyssa Really? What ²_____ (she / do) there?

Kyle Well, she ³_____ (work) as an English teacher for three months in Peru. Then she ⁴_____ (travel) around Chile and Argentina.

Alyssa And ⁵_____ (she / change) as a result of the experience? She was quite naive before she ⁶_____ (go), in my opinion.

Kyle She looks different. She ⁷_____ (not have) her hair cut since before she left!

Alyssa ⁸_____ (she / meet) anybody while she ⁹_____ (travel)? A boyfriend, I mean.

Kyle Yes. While she ¹⁰_____ (work) at the school in Peru, she ¹¹_____ (start) going out with one of the other young teachers. He ¹²_____ (live) in Lima for a year before she arrived, so he showed her around.

Alyssa And is she still in touch with him?

Kyle No, she isn't. Something weird ¹³_____ (happen) in Argentina. She ¹⁴_____ (not want) to tell me about it, but I ¹⁵_____ (insist)!

Alyssa What? Tell me!

●●●●●● CHALLENGE! ●●●●●●●

Continue the dialogue. Write another four lines, two for each speaker. Use exercise 2 to give you ideas.

Kyle _____

Alyssa _____

Kyle _____

Alyssa _____

 Extra Practice

1C CULTURE
Worst Britons

I can express my opinions on well-known people.

Revision: Student's Book page 7

1 Complete the summary with the words in the box.

> celebrities   commentators   figures   poll
> Prime Minister   public   votes

In 2002, the BBC conducted a ¹_____ to discover which famous Britons were considered to be the greatest of all time by the general ²_____. In first place on the list was Winston Churchill, who was Britain's ³_____ during the Second World War (1939–45). Churchill received around half of all the ⁴_____. Some social ⁵_____ were surprised that none of the top ten was alive. This showed that, while many people are interested in ⁶_____, they do not regard them as equal to great ⁷_____ from history.

2 Read the text about the 100 Worst Britons. Which of the following are definitely on the list?

doctors ☐   film stars ☐   high court judges ☐
lawyers ☐   members of the royal family ☐
politicians ☐   reality TV contestants ☐
singers ☐   TV presenters ☐

3 Are these sentences true or false? Write T or F.

1 People who were in prison could not vote in the Channel 4 100 *Worst Britons* poll. ____

2 Jade Goody won the reality TV show *Big Brother*. ____

3 Seven former *Pop Idol* contestants are in the list. ____

4 The list suggests that TV presenters are not popular with the British public. ____

5 The text suggests Queen Elizabeth II is unpopular because of her role, not her personality. ____

6 The text suggests Richard Branson is unpopular because people are jealous of his success. ____

●●●●●● CHALLENGE! ●●●●●●

Choose two famous, living people from your country that you would put in a list of 100 Worst Celebrities. Explain why you have chosen them.

1ˢᵗ person: (name) _____

reason _____

2ˢᵗ person: (name) _____

reason _____

100 Worst Britons

In 2003, a year after the BBC's poll to discover the 100 greatest Britons, Channel 4 allowed viewers to vote for the 100 worst Britons. Unlike the BBC, Channel 4 did not allow votes for people who were not alive at the time of the poll. They also excluded people who were in prison or awaiting trial.

Many of the people in the list of *100 Greatest Britons* are there because of significant achievements in the world of science, music, literature and exploration. Many of those in the *100 Worst Britons* list are there precisely because, in the opinion of the voters, they haven't achieved anything worthwhile but are nonetheless in the public eye. Number 4 in the list, Jade Goody, became famous for appearing in the reality TV show, *Big Brother*. And although the Reality TV show, *Pop Idol* has been a huge hit in the UK, it provides the list with no fewer than seven people, including judges, presenters and former contestants. And judging by the list, the British public has a particular dislike for TV presenters and politicians.

Most interesting are the people who appear in both the *100 Greatest* list and the *100 Worst* list. These are controversial figures who have large numbers of supporters but who are also detested by large numbers of people. Two former Prime Ministers fall into this category: Tony Blair and Margaret Thatcher. Two singers also appear on both lists: Cliff Richard, who first became a pop star in the 1950s and is still performing, and Robbie Williams, who has millions of fans worldwide but whose personality many people find arrogant. The reigning monarch, Queen Elizabeth II, appears as number 10 on the list of greatest Britons and number 24 on the list of worst Britons. This might be a reflection of the public's attitude to the monarchy as an institution, rather than the personality of the Queen herself. Entrepreneur and adventurer, Richard Branson is on both lists, too. Many people admire his energy and achievements, building successful companies in the fields of air travel, music, publishing, mobile phones and even space tourism. However, many people also dislike his public image and his frequent publicity stunts.

In fact, looking at the list as a whole, being in the public eye too much seems to be the main cause of disapproval. Although he is a hero for many young footballers, number 91 on the list of 100 Worst Britons is David Beckham – and his wife, Victoria, is number 13.

Revision: Student's Book page 8–9

1 Complete the table of related nouns and adjectives.

noun	adjective
horror	1 _____
2 _____	relieved
obstinacy	3 _____
4 _____	determined
resignation	5 _____
6 _____	miserable

2 Rewrite the sentences using verbs in the box.

clamber   deteriorate   drift   grab   pour
rot   sob

1 Water was flowing into the boat very quickly.
_____

2 With difficulty, we climbed onto the rocks.
_____

3 The wooden floor was so old and damp that it had fallen apart.
_____

4 The little boy was crying noisily and pointing to his sister's ice cream.
_____

5 A thief suddenly took hold of my bag and ran off.
_____

6 He dropped a leaf into the water and watched it move slowly under the bridge.
_____

7 As she got older, her health got worse.
_____

3 Read the text, *Trouble at Sea*, quickly. In what way could you describe Violet Jessop as both very unlucky and very lucky?

She was unlucky because _____
_____

She was lucky because _____
_____

4 Choose from sentences A–G the sentence which fits each gap (1–6). There is one sentence that you do not need.

A Initially, she worked with the Royal Mail Line like her mother, but later moved to a company called White Star.

B Violet wrote that she was lying in bed but not quite asleep when the collision occurred.

C That is why she decided not to accept another job on a large passenger ship.

D But even at this early age, Violet was a survivor and recovered fully from her illness.

E She was sucked under the boat and hit her head on the keel, but she survived.

F Both ships were badly damaged, but managed to struggle back to port.

G It was so badly damaged that it sank, with the loss of 30 members of the crew.

5 Find these words and phrases in the text. There is one in each paragraph.

Paragraph 1: a phrase meaning 'personally' (3 words)
_____

Paragraph 2: a serious disease _____

Paragraph 3: a female member of a ship's crew _____

Paragraph 4: a word that means 'very good' _____

Paragraph 5: a phrase meaning a new ship's first voyage (2 words) _____

Paragraph 6: a bomb that is hidden in the sea _____

Paragraph 7: the period of life when you have finished working _____

●●●●●● **CHALLENGE!** ●●●●●●

Imagine that you were one of the survivors of the Titanic who escaped in a lifeboat. Write a short text saying what you saw and how you felt.

_____
_____
_____
_____
_____
_____
_____
_____
_____
_____
_____
_____

Trouble at Sea

Most people never experience at first hand the fear and excitement of a disaster at sea. Violet Jessop experienced it three times! She did not go looking for danger, but reading the story of her life, it sometimes seems that danger came looking for her.

Violet was born in Argentina, the first of six children born to Irish emigrants, William and Katherine Jessop. Her father was a sheep farmer. As a child, Violet became very ill with tuberculosis, and her doctor told her parents that she would die within weeks. [1]_____

The death of her father led the family to return to Britain, where her mother needed to work to provide an income. She found a job as a stewardess for the Royal Mail Line, a shipping company, while Violet and her brothers and sisters went to live at a convent school. When her mother had to stop work because of poor health, Violet gave up school to became a stewardess herself. [2]_____ Violet didn't want to work for White Star because their ships sailed across the North Atlantic and often encountered bad weather. Nevertheless, Violet became a stewardess for the White Star Line working 17 hours a day for less than £3 a month. She was serving on board the Olympic when it collided with HMS Hawke in 1911. [3]_____

Violet was quite happy working on the Olympic and didn't really want to join the Titanic, another ship owned by the same company. However, her friends persuaded her that working on the largest passenger ship in the world would be a wonderful experience.

Violet Jessop's own account of the Titanic's maiden voyage talks about a translated Hebrew prayer that an old Irish woman had given her. The prayer was supposed to protect her against fire and water. Violet, who was a devout Catholic, read the prayer as she relaxed in her cabin only hours before the Titanic sank. [4]_____ Immediately, she was ordered to go on deck. As water poured into the ship and it began to sink, she helped a group of women into a lifeboat, and after eight hours in the boat, Violet and the others were rescued by another ship. About 1500 other passengers were not so lucky: they died in the tragedy.

When the Great War broke out in 1914, Violet served as a nurse with the British Red Cross on board a ship called the Britannic. As a medical ship, the Britannic was safe from enemy attack because of an international agreement. However, towards the end of 1916, the ship collided with a mine in the Aegean Sea. [5]_____ At the time of the collision, Violet herself was on deck and was thrown over the side of the ship into the sea by the force of the explosion. [6]_____ She was picked up out of the water and taken to safety. Years later, a doctor told her that she had actually fractured her skull in the accident.

Despite these three separate incidents, Violet Jessop continued to work at sea for another 34 years. She retired in 1950 and enjoyed many years of retirement before her death in 1971 at the age of 84.

Past perfect simple and continuous

I can talk about actions and events and their consequences in the past.

1 Look at the time line. Then complete the text using the past perfect continuous with *for* or *since*.

1990
Boy band Take That
(Robbie Williams,
Gary Barlow, Howard Donald,
Mark Owen and Jason Orange)
start performing together

1992
Take That start
having hits

1996
Take That split up

1998
Gary Barlow starts
writing songs for
other performers

2000
Howard Donald becomes
a DJ in Germany

2001
Jason Orange becomes
a psychology student

2004
Mark Owen starts
running his own record
label

2006
Take That reunite without
Robbie Williams for a hugely
successful world tour

By the time Take That started having hits, they (perform / for) _had been performing together for two years._ When they split up in 1996, they (have hits / since) ¹ _____ _____. They got back together in 2006. Gary Barlow (write songs / since) ² _____ _____. Howard Donald (work as a DJ / for) ³ _____. Jason Orange (study psychology / for) ⁴ _____ _____ and Mark Owen (run record label / since) ⁵ _____ _____.

2 Yesterday, Ava began an expedition to climb Mount Everest. Had she completed her preparation schedule?
Write sentences in the past perfect simple, affirmative or negative.

> gain 6 kilos in weight ✔
> complete a physical training regime ✔
> study basic Nepalese ✘
> obtain long-term weather forecasts ✔
> plan a route to the summit ✔
> get to know the other climbers in the group ✘
> spend a week at high altitude ✔

She had gained 6 kilos in weight.

1 _____
2 _____
3 _____
4 _____
5 _____
6 _____

3 Study the verbs below. Tick the verbs which are not usually used in continuous tenses (state verbs).

belong ☐
enjoy ☐
know ☐
imagine ☐
spend ☐
think ☐
understand ☐
wait ☐

4 Complete the sentences with the past perfect simple or continuous of the verbs from exercise 3.

1 Nothing Tara did surprised him, because he _____ her well since childhood.
2 She was glad when the bus arrived, as she _____ more than half an hour in the cold.
3 We were sad when the concert ended, because we _____ it so much.
4 I was amazed when Fran phoned, because I _____ about her just a minute earlier.
5 When he finished speaking, I realised that I _____ only a fraction of what he'd said.
6 The bracelet was particularly precious to her because it _____ to her grandmother.
7 I was a little disappointed when I saw the hotel room because I _____ something bigger.
8 Her parents decided that she _____ too much time with her boyfriend.

 Extra Practice

Talking about photos

I can talk about a given topic illustrated by photos.

1 🎧 01 Complete the extract from the Speaking exam. Then listen and check.

as though	connected	hard	imagine	judging
say	show	like	would guess	

'The photos are ¹_____ with the topic of school. Both photos ²_____ students in class. In the first photo I ³_____ that they're about 13 years old. It looks ⁴_____ a science lesson, and ⁵_____ by the students' expressions, I'd ⁶_____ that they are enjoying their lesson. They look interested and it looks ⁷_____ they are working hard. Most of them are looking at the experiment and working together. They are all wearing uniform – it's quite an old-fashioned-looking uniform, so I ⁸_____ that it's a private school, but it could be a state school. It's ⁹_____ to say.'

2 🎧 02 Order the words to make sentences about the second photo. Then listen to the speaker and check your answers.

1 they I are years 17 reckon old about
_____
_____

2 mixed of girls it's and class a boys
_____
_____

3 to tell what it's of difficult lesson in they're kind
_____
_____

4 it they're be lesson in that maths could a
_____
_____

5 as is one if looks them it asleep of
_____
_____

6 clear front the in that the interested it's girl desk isn't
_____
_____

3 Write about these photos, comparing and contrasting them. Use phrases from exercises 1 and 2.

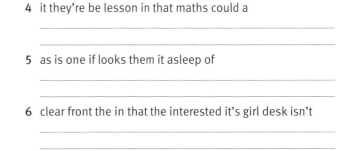

●●●●●● **CHALLENGE!** ●●●●●●●

Can you explain what these quotations about education mean? Use your own words.

1 'The roots of education are bitter, but the fruits are sweet.' *Aristotle*
_____
_____

2 'Education is what remains when you have forgotten everything you learned in school.' *Einstein*
_____
_____
_____

1G WRITING Magazine article

I can write a magazine article giving an account of an event.

Preparation

1 Read the jumbled parts of an article. Match the paragraphs (A–D) with the paragraph plan below.

A I'd been staying with my aunt and uncle at their house near the sea. The weather had been fantastic, and I'd been going to the beach every day for a swim. There was a large, flat rock about five hundred metres out to sea, and I enjoyed swimming out to it. I'd even started timing myself to see how quickly I could get there.

B When I finally reached safety, I was so relieved. It felt as if I'd been swimming for ever. If the distance had been twenty metres further, I wouldn't have made it. I'd never been so exhausted in my life! After that day, I always checked the times of the tides before I went swimming!

C This is something that happened to me about three years ago. At the time, I wasn't really frightened, but looking back, it was quite a dangerous incident. In fact, in some ways, I was lucky to survive.

D One afternoon, I swam to the rock as usual and climbed onto it for a rest, as it was a warm and sunny day. I was so tired that I fell asleep. Only when I woke up did I realise that the tide was coming in – and fast! The rock was now more than a kilometre out to sea! Could I swim that far? I wasn't sure, but I had no choice. I dived into the sea and started swimming.

Paragraph 1: Introduction _____

Paragraph 2: Background information _____

Paragraph 3: Main events _____

Paragraph 4: Conclusion _____

2 Find at least one example in the article of:

1 a sequencing word or phrase

_____

2 a phrase or sentence followed by an exclamation mark

_____

3 an extreme adjective

_____

4 stylistic inversion

_____

3 Rewrite the highlighted sentences from the article using stylistic inversion. Begin like this:

1 Had _____

2 Never _____

3 So _____

4 Think of something that happened to you which was dangerous or frightening. Make notes.

Where were you? _____

What happened? _____

_____

When did it happen? _____

Who was involved? _____

How did you feel? _____

5 Use your notes from exercise 4 to write an article about the event. Follow the paragraph plan from exercise 1.

Writing Guide

1 Write a brief introduction saying where and when the event happened. Don't go into detail at this stage.

2 Explain the background to the event. Say why you were there, what you had been doing, etc.

3 Describe what happened. Remember that the past simple is the most commonly used tense for this kind of narration.

4 Write a brief conclusion. Say what you learned from the event and how it affected you.

CHECKLIST

Have you:
• followed the paragraph plan?
• used appropriate tenses for each part of the article?
• used stylistic inversion or a feature from exercise 2?
• checked your work for mistakes?

 Extra Practice

2 For what it's worth

A VOCABULARY
Value and price

I can talk about money and finance.

1 Complete the chart with adjectives made from the nouns.

1	price	6	economy
2	price	7	profit
3	worth	8	value
4	finance	9	worth
5	cost	10	economy

[Crossword grid with numbered cells 1–10]

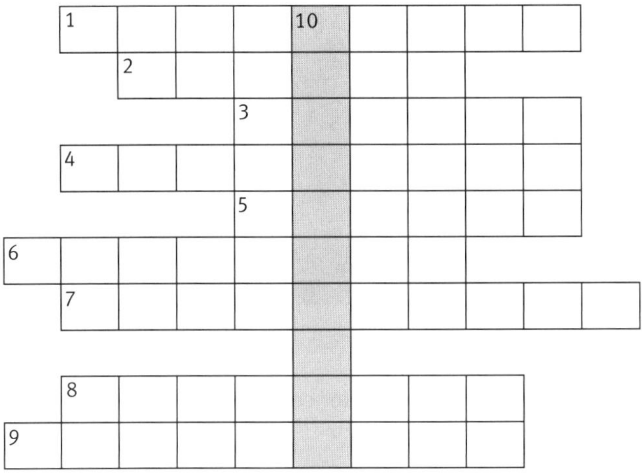

2 Choose the correct adjective.

1 We're spending too much money. We need to be more **economic / economical**.
2 The food at that restaurant is great, but it's very **pricey / precious**.
3 The website provides **valuable / profitable** advice on choosing the right university course.
4 Economists are predicting that rising interest rates will create **economical / financial** chaos.
5 I thought the painting I inherited from my grandmother was worth a lot of money, but it turned out to be **worthless / precious**.
6 Businesses often prefer to sell goods on the Internet, because it is more **profitable / valuable**.
7 A **worthy / priceless** collection of Michelangelo drawings was destroyed in the fire.
8 At the end of the last century we experienced a period of rapid **profitable / economic** growth.
9 They wanted to buy a house in London, but it would have proved too **costly / over-priced**.
10 Trying to improve the lives of poor people is a **valuable / worthy** ambition for any politician.
11 In my opinion DVDs and CDs are ridiculously **overpriced / valuable**.
12 This necklace isn't worth a great deal but it's very **worthy / precious** as it belonged to my mother.

Extra Practice

● ● ● ● ● **Extension:** Expressions connected with money

3 Match a–j with 1–10 to make expressions connected with money.

a	be dirt	1	aside
b	cost	2	somebody off
c	rip	3	a killing
d	pay through	4	the nose (for something)
e	make	5	cheap
f	tighten	6	a fortune
g	put	7	off
h	be well	8	your belt
i	splash	9	hard up
j	be	10	out (on something)

4 Rewrite the sentences using expressions from exercise 3.

1 The skiing holiday was great but it cost a lot of money.
_____
2 Jason paid far too much for his new car.
_____
3 They haven't had much money since Sam lost his job.
_____
4 We spent a lot of money on a new computer.
_____
5 Sarah got a bonus at work, which she's going to save for the future.
_____
6 Nowadays printers hardly cost anything.
_____
7 I think you were charged far too much by the garage.
_____
8 We'll have to economise to avoid getting into debt.
_____

● ● ● ● ● ● **CHALLENGE!** ● ● ● ● ● ● ●

Write sentences using the words given.

1 afford _____
2 be worth _____
3 change (*verb*) _____
4 cost (*verb*) _____
5 owe _____
6 value (*verb*)_____

2B GRAMMAR
Determiners

I can use determiners to describe quantities.

1 Complete the news article with *a/an*, *the* or no article.

¹_____ Crime Doesn't Pay

Jane Wilson only had a few pounds in ²_____ bank, so she decided to limit herself to ³_____ £10 cash withdrawal. But when she went to the ATM to withdraw ⁴_____ money, she discovered to her amazement that she had £100,000 in her account. Jane was used to living on £100 ⁵_____ week, but over ⁶_____ next few days ⁷_____ 25-year-old lived the life of ⁸_____ lottery winner, even though she knew the money wasn't hers. She splashed out on ⁹_____ thousands of pounds worth of ¹⁰_____ clothes, took out nearly £10,000 in ¹¹_____ cash and booked ¹²_____ luxury holiday to ¹³_____ USA. She also spent money on her family and gave ¹⁴_____ money to a charity that helps ¹⁵_____

disabled. However, ¹⁶_____ staff at ¹⁷_____ bank soon realised their mistake and froze Jane's account. She knew there was no point in running away, so she stayed at ¹⁸_____ home and waited for ¹⁹_____ police to knock on ²⁰_____ door. In court she pleaded guilty to stealing the money and was given a two-year suspended sentence.

2 Choose the correct option: *some*, *any* or nothing.

1 Peter hasn't got **some** / **any** / --- long hair.
2 Can I have **some** / **any** / --- grapes, please?
3 I haven't got **some** / **any** / --- money in the bank.
4 I don't like **some** / **any** / --- strong cheese.
5 Call me at **some** / **any** / --- time. It doesn't matter when.
6 What **some** / **any** / --- beautiful flowers!
7 **Some** / **Any** / --- cars use a lot of petrol, others are more economical.
8 **Some** / **Any** / --- train from this platform goes to Hastings.

3 Complete the sentences with *few*, *a few*, *little* or *a little*.

1 It usually snows a lot here in the winter but last year there was very _____ snow.
2 I bought this jacket _____ days ago.
3 I've run out of bread. Could you give me _____?
4 Sam's determined to leave school. There's _____ use in trying to change his mind.
5 _____ tourists visit the Arctic. It's dangerous.
6 Sorry I'm late. I lost my way _____ times coming here.
7 _____ people stay in this hotel because it's ridiculously expensive.
8 I don't understand this. I need _____ help.

4 Complete or write a sentence so that it means the same as the first sentence. Include the word in brackets.

1 It doesn't matter which road you take. (any)
You can _take any_____ road.
2 We don't have a lot of time. (much)
We _____
3 My brother plays football and so do I. (both)
My _____
4 It didn't rain on Tuesday and it didn't rain on Wednesday. (either ... or)
It _____
5 The shops are all closed. (none)
_____ open.
6 The food wasn't good. And it wasn't cheap. (neither ... nor)
The food _____
7 There aren't any easy answers. (no)
_____
8 Not many of my relatives live nearby. (few)
_____
9 My parents haven't got much money. (little)
_____
10 He read the magazine from beginning to end. (whole)
_____
11 The majority of graduates quickly find a job. (most)
_____
12 All of us want to be happy. (every)
_____

Extra Practice

2C CULTURE
Buying abroad

I can talk about British emigration.

Revision: Student's Book page 17

1 Complete the sentences with words from the box.

basement	conversion	detached	lease
open-plan	period	top-floor	unfurnished

1 The flat we live in was _____ so we had to buy furniture.

2 We live in a _____ house. Our nearest neighbour is 100 metres away.

3 Sally recently moved into a new barn _____. Until last year the building was part of a farm.

4 I don't like _____ houses. I prefer to have separate rooms.

5 We live in the _____ flat, so when you arrive go down the steps.

6 Tom's home looks like a _____ cottage, but in fact it was only built five years ago.

7 We have fabulous views across the city from our _____ flat.

8 We have a 12-month _____ on our house.

2 Read the text quickly. Which paragraph (A–D) tells you about:

1 which countries UK emigrants go to? _____

2 why people choose to emigrate? _____

3 future emigration? _____

3 Are the sentences true or false? Write T or F.

1 About 600,000 Britons live abroad permanently or for part of the year. _____

2 The top six destinations are other English-speaking countries. _____

3 The majority of emigrants are middle-aged. _____

4 Some people emigrate to find somewhere cheaper to live. _____

5 Emigrants can't usually afford to buy property. _____

4 Express information from the text using these numbers.

1 500,000 _____

_____

2 1,300,000 _____

_____

3 750,000 _____

_____

4 1,000,000 _____

_____

Leaving Britain

A Every three minutes someone in Britain boards a plane or a ferry and travels abroad to start a new life. Emigration from the UK has increased dramatically over the past 10 years and now at least five and half million British citizens live permanently overseas. It is estimated that a further 500,000 Britons spend part of the year abroad, either spending extended periods in second homes, or working. This means that 10% of British people are living abroad at any one time.

B Six of the eight most popular destinations for Britons seeking a new life abroad are other English-speaking countries: Australia (with 1.3 million expatriates), the US (0.7 million), Canada (0.6 million), Ireland (0.3 million), and New Zealand and South Africa (each with about 0.2 million). The second most popular country overall, however, is Spain, where three quarters of a million British people have settled permanently.

C Why do so many people choose to leave the UK and settle abroad? The majority are either young people without families, who are just starting their careers, or people at the end of their working life who are seeking to retire. Other reasons for emigrating are to find a better climate, better quality of life (many complain that the UK is too expensive), or to join other family members who've already left the UK. Whatever the reason, cheap air travel and free movement within the European Union mean that emigrating is easier than ever. Moreover, high property prices in the UK mean that people can exchange a fairly modest house in the UK for something much grander overseas.

D It is predicted that a further one million Britons will leave in the next five years. So, has this led to a decline in the UK population? No, because for every two people who emigrate, three people move to the UK from abroad.

Revision: Student's Book page 18–19

1 Complete the sentences using the words in the box.

cut down	equivalent	income	poverty	rent
run out of	spend	waste		

1 I've _____ money. Can I borrow some from you?
2 A shocking 37 million Americans live in _____ , according to a recent report.
3 Credit cards tempt some people to _____ more than they earn.
4 The _____ for the flat we live in comes to £500 a month.
5 In 1850, a slave in the American South cost the _____ of £25,000 in today's money.
6 The government has _____ expenditure on health and education.
7 Don't _____ your money on expensive designer clothes that you don't need.
8 Of the Earth's six billion people, half live on an _____ of under $2 a day.

2 Read the text, ignoring the gaps. Answer the questions.

1 Which other two famous works by Orwell are mentioned in the text?

_____ and _____

2 In which city did Orwell work in a hotel?

_____

3 Why couldn't he find work in London at first?

_____

3 Match sentences A–G with gaps 1–6. There is one sentence that you do not need.

A He recounts how this life had a severe effect on his humanity.
B Having found a job and started to earn some money, life improved dramatically for him.
C However, when this work dried up, he had to start selling his possessions while he tried to search for more work.
D Until his boss returns, he finds himself sleeping on the streets of the city with the other poor and unemployed.
E Still I can point to one or two things I have definitely learned by being hard up.
F He finds himself working seventeen and a half hours a day in the restaurant, almost without a break.
G However, Orwell was also completely against totalitarianism in any form.

4 Are the sentences true or false? (The answers may be in the sentences in exercise 3.) Write T or F.

1 *Down and Out in Paris and London* is an exact account of Orwell's experiences in the two cities. ____
2 Orwell took a job in a hotel because he was fed up of teaching and writing. ____
3 He earned very little money working in the hotel. ____
4 One night Orwell couldn't sleep because someone was killed near his room. ____
5 Orwell slept outside in the open in both Paris and London. ____
6 Orwell thought that it was the workers' own fault that they had such dreadful working conditions. ____
7 Orwell had a lot of sympathy for tramps and beggars. ____
8 Orwell thought that socialism was good as long as it didn't turn into totalitarianism. ____

●●●●●● CHALLENGE! ●●●●●●

Imagine that you are homeless and unemployed. Write a short text saying how you find food, where you sleep, and how you feel.

_____
_____
_____
_____
_____
_____
_____
_____
_____
_____
_____
_____
_____
_____
_____
_____
_____
_____
_____
_____
_____
_____
_____
_____
_____
_____
_____

Down and out in Paris and London

George Orwell is one of Britain's best-known authors of the 20th century, responsible for such famous works as *Animal Farm* and *Nineteen Eighty-Four*. However, there was a period in his life when things didn't go so well for him.

Down and Out in Paris and London is Orwell's semi-autobiographical account of living in poverty in both cities. The narrative begins in Paris where Orwell lived for two years, attempting to make a living by giving English lessons and writing reviews and articles for magazines. [1]_____ After days without food, he finally found a hotel job with his Russian friend, Boris. There he ended up working long hours as a dishwasher and kitchen assistant in a hotel, where he earned barely enough to survive.

He describes his routine life as one of the working poor in Paris as: slaving then sleeping, slaving then sleeping, then drinking on a Saturday night through to Sunday morning, which briefly made his life seem bearable. [2]_____ He describes a murder which happened just outside his window, and says 'The thing that strikes me in looking back, is that I was in bed and asleep within three minutes of the murder ... We were working people and where was the sense of wasting sleep over murder?'

In the hope of a better job and more money, Orwell moves to working in a restaurant, but the owner doesn't pay him for ten days and so he is reduced to sleeping on a park bench rather than facing his landlady over non-payment of rent. [3]_____ He blames the dreadful existence of his fellow workers for turning them all into zombies: '[They have] been trapped by a routine which makes thought impossible. If [they] thought at all they would long ago have ... gone on strike for better treatment. But they do not think, because they have no leisure for it; their life has made slaves of them.'

Orwell travels to London having been promised that a job is waiting for him. However, he can't start work because his new employer has gone on holiday. [4]_____

At the end of the book, Orwell summed up what he had learned from his experience of living in poverty: 'At present I do not feel that I have seen more than the fringe of poverty. [5]_____ I shall never again think that all tramps are drunken scoundrels, nor expect a beggar to be grateful when I give him a penny, nor be surprised if men out of work lack energy.'

These experiences led Orwell to strengthen his democratic socialist beliefs. He blamed wealthy people for being ignorant of the reality of poverty. He said that the rich were afraid of the poor: they didn't want to give them freedom from poverty, because they thought that the poor would then threaten their own way of life. [6]_____ His subsequent novels, *Animal Farm* and *Nineteen Eighty-Four*, depict worlds where people in authority have gone horribly out of control. He showed us how difficult it is to make a fair and just society, but he didn't want the human race to stop trying.

1 Complete the text. Use the infinitive or *-ing* form of the verbs in brackets.

Lotto FORUM

[LOGON] [POST ARTIICLE] [REPLY]

I can't bear [1] _____ (listen) to lottery winners who insist that they will carry on [2] _____ (live) in exactly the same way as they did before. Although they may really hope [3] _____ (continue) their lives unchanged, I admit to [4] _____ (have) a serious problem believing them. If they hadn't intended [5] _____ (change) their lives at all, then why on earth did they want [6] _____ (buy) a lottery ticket in the first place? Suddenly receiving a lot of money, when you had none before, can't fail [7] _____ (have) a huge effect on anybody's life. Lottery winners who propose [8] _____ (give away) ALL of their winnings are very rare indeed. And once you decide [9] _____ (spend) a lot of money on something – a big new house, for example – you will become a different person. It's unavoidable, no matter who you are. But if there are any lottery winners who are having difficulty [10] _____ (deal with) their new riches, then they are welcome to give some of their money to me!

---

2 Write the correct form of the verb.

1 a I remember _____ (send) Jim a birthday card though he says he didn't receive it.

　b Please remember _____ (lock) the door when you leave the house.

2 a I regret _____ (tell) you that you've lost your place in the volleyball team.

　b I regretted _____ (tell) my parents that I'd decided not to study medicine.

3 a We drove all day, stopping only _____ (have) lunch at a service station.

　b Will you please stop _____ (criticise) me.

4 a Despite losing an arm in an accident, Fred went on _____ (play) football.

　b George studied languages and went on _____ (teach) French.

5 a I tried _____ (take) the bus to work but it was always overcrowded.

　b The thief tried _____ (take) my credit card but I stopped him.

3 Rewrite the sentences using the verb in brackets.

1 I told Mike that he should get an early night. (advise)
　I advised Mike to get an early night.

2 I said I would give Jenny a lift into town. (agree)
　_____
　_____

3 It was easy for me to repair the broken vase. (have difficulty)
　_____
　_____

4 Dad told me I couldn't stay out late. (let)
　_____
　_____

5 We're thinking about selling our car. (consider)
　_____
　_____

6 I think it's really nice to relax in front of the TV in the evening. (enjoy)
　_____
　_____

7 I finally succeeded in solving the crossword. (manage)
　_____
　_____

8 I told Millie not to forget to bring some CDs to the party. (remind)
　_____
　_____

● ● ● ● ● ● CHALLENGE! ● ● ● ● ● ●

Write true sentences using the verbs in the box followed by another verb in the correct form.

can't stand	fail	fancy	hope	let	keep on

1 _____
2 _____
3 _____
4 _____
5 _____
6 _____

 Extra Practice

SPEAKING

Discussing pros and cons

I can present the pros and cons of a statement in a discussion.

1 Put the words in the correct order to make phrases for trying to persuade another person. Add punctuation.

1 admit / you / to / have / that

_____

2 agree / but / wouldn't / that / you

_____

3 at / look / it / way / well / this

_____

4 think / just / about

_____

5 with / there's / but / nothing / surely / wrong

_____

6 that / you / deny / can't

_____

2 Complete the phrases for discussing pros and cons using the words in the box.

benefit	consequences	creates	disadvantages
drawbacks	favour	for	other	positive
several	thing		

Pros

The main ¹_____ of ... is ...

... is generally a good ²_____ because ...

... has ³_____ things in its ⁴_____.

... produces some ⁵_____ effects – for example, ...

Cons

On the ⁶_____ hand, ...

As ⁷_____ the ⁸_____, ...

But there are ⁹_____ too.

However, it also ¹⁰_____ problems.

But some of the ¹¹_____ are less attractive.

3 🎧 03 Listen. Which question from 1–4 below are the students discussing?

1 What are the pros and cons of shopping in shops? ☐

2 What are the advantages of online shopping? ☐

3 What personal experience, if any, do you have of online shopping? ☐

4 What are the pros and cons of online shopping? ☐

4 🎧 03 The following phrases can be used to introduce both pros and cons. Listen again and tick those that the student used.

Introducing the first argument

One advantage/disadvantage of ... is (that) ... ☐

The most obvious advantage/disadvantage of ... is (that) ... ☐

One positive/negative aspect of ... is (that) ... ☐

... is/isn't a good idea because ... ☐

Introducing subsequent arguments

Another advantage/disadvantage is (that) ... ☐

Not only that but ... ☐

Another important point is that ... ☐

An even stronger argument for/against ... is (that) ... ☐

5 Write a short paragraph giving two more advantages of online shopping and two more disadvantages. Use phrases from exercises 2 and 4 to introduce them. Use the ideas in the box to help you or invent your own.

Pros

shop 24 hours a day   convenient   stay at home wider choice   compare prices   gifts for people who live a long way from you   buy things from anywhere in the world

Cons

identity theft   genuine website?   goods out of stock delivery charges   complaining   returning faulty goods   speaking to real people

_____

_____

_____

_____

_____

_____

_____

_____

_____

_____

_____

_____

_____

_____

_____

_____

Essay: for and against

I can present the arguments for and against in an essay.

Preparation

1 Match 1–6 with a–f. Underline the words and phrases that express contrast.

1 I don't believe that money makes you happy. ☐
2 Much as I would like to be rich, ☐
3 Having money can remove a lot of everyday worries. ☐
4 Many people are happy, ☐
5 The love of money is the root of much evil, ☐
6 The love of money makes people commit crime. ☐

a Nevertheless, it would be unfair to argue that money is the sole cause of crime.
b in spite of the fact that they haven't got much money.
c On the contrary, I think that money is often the cause of great unhappiness.
d it wouldn't necessarily make me happier.
e However, it can't solve all our problems.
f whereas money itself is not.

2 You are going to write an essay entitled: *Money is the root of all evil. Discuss.* Make notes for an introduction. Use these ideas to help you, or think of your own.

> It's a very old saying.
> How does money cause evil?
> We can't live without money.
> Fair to blame money for all evil? One of many causes?

3 Complete the phrases with the words in the box.

> argued   hand   However   maintain   important
> one   opposite

Presenting one side of the argument

Firstly, it's ¹_____ to state that …
On the ²_____ hand, …
It is sometimes ³_____ that …
Moreover, … / Furthermore, … / What is more, …

Presenting the other side of the argument

⁴_____, …
On the other ⁵_____, …
Some people take the ⁶_____ view, and claim /
⁷_____ that …
Moreover, … / Furthermore, … / What is more, …

4 Think of points that you could include, and write at least three under each of these headings.

Pros

Money makes people commit crime.
_____
_____
_____
_____

Cons

_____
_____
_____
_____

5 Decide whether, in your opinion, the pros or the cons are stronger arguments, and why. You will express this opinion in the final paragraph. Use these phrases to help you.

> On balance, …
> To sum up, I would say that …
> While it's true that …, I firmly believe that …
> Some people feel strongly that … . However, I believe …
> It can be argued that …
> It's true to say that … . Nevertheless, …

6 Write your essay, following the writing guide below.

Writing Guide

Paragraph 1
Introduction. Some background information.
Paragraph 2
Two or three arguments for, with examples.
Paragraph 3
Two or three arguments against, with examples.
Paragraph 4
Summary and your opinion.

CHECKLIST

Have you:
• written 200–250 words?
• followed the writing guide?
• included phrases for introducing arguments?
• checked your work for mistakes?

Extra Practice

EXAM TASK – Reading

Read the text. Then read statements 1–8 and find the paragraph (A–D) in the text which contains information about them. Write the correct letter in the table. Finally, decide if the statements are true (T) or false (F).

The Importance of Money

A

A great philosopher once said 'Money is a barrier against all possible evils.' Money can prevent the sufferings that come with poverty like cold and hunger. Even though sickness cannot be totally obliterated by money, it can be considerably relieved by it. Giving away money to charity can also provide us with the satisfaction of relieving others from suffering. With money, we can obtain an advanced education that may aid us in the development of genius and extraordinary achievements. It gives us the leisure to devote a part of our time to culture and art. Money can provide a powerful diversion for all our troubles by permitting distraction from the anxieties that assail us.

B

So we must try to get a thorough understanding of all that we may possibly do, in an honourable and legitimate way, to conserve wealth. Even to those who have inherited wealth, idleness can be a certain cause of ruin. A great fortune needs genuine labour for efficient administration. Those who leave this duty to strangers may pay a penalty for their negligence. This is why a rich man, who wants to preserve and increase his fortune, should be his own business manager.

C

Even artists must know the price that their work is worth. It is necessary for the artist to be a businessman in order to have the right to be a genius. History is full of examples of this. The great Shakespeare laboured as a theatre manager to obtain the necessary leisure to produce his dramatic masterpieces. Edison worked as a telegraph operator to pay the bills while he 'moonlighted' as an inventor.

D

From the bottom to the top of the ladder, it is necessary to amass money in order to apply it to some great cause. Money is the means by which we may fulfil our purpose in a larger and better way. Everyone should, in his own way, make an effort to amass some money. Some will apply money to their daily wants. Others seek to swell the fortune that they desire to leave to their children. Some only desire money so they can devote it to some noble enterprise or charity. Finally, a large number see money chiefly as a means of immediate gratification.

		True/False	A–D
1	You cannot buy health.		
2	You have to work hard to manage your finances.		
3	Creative people don't need to be skilful in business and financial matters.		
4	Giving money to those worse off than you offers its own reward.		
5	People can have very different reasons for accumulating wealth.		
6	Money cannot distract us from our worries.		
7	Everyone, however rich, should take care of their own money.		
8	Some people save money for future generations.		

EXAM TASK – Use of English

Complete the text with the correct form of the words in brackets.

After three decades of being either endangered or threatened, America's bald eagle, its symbol of
1_____ (PROUD), has made a
2_____ (REMARK) comeback. In June the U.S. took the high-flying bird off the Endangered Species Act's 'threatened' list.

For a century (1870–1970) bald eagle populations, which used to inhabit 3_____ (MOUNTAIN) areas of the United States, 4_____ (SEVERE) declined because of hunting, habitat
5_____ (LOSE) and the use of DDT. In 1963, there were only 417 breeding pairs. By 1970, people feared it was facing near 6_____ (EXTINCT). Further problems, such as habitat destruction, food-
7_____ (CONTAMINATE), and
8_____ (LEGAL) shooting raised concerns.

Now, there are 9,789 breeding pairs in the United States, all of which are protected under the Bald and Golden Eagle 9_____ (PROTECT) Act, which prohibits anyone without a permit from shooting, poisoning, wounding, killing, capturing, trapping, collecting, molesting and disturbing bald eagles.

While the eagles have made a 10_____ (SUCCESS) return, there are still 541 animals in the United States listed as threatened or endangered under the Endangered Species Act.

🎧04 You will hear four teenagers talking about their achievements. Read the statements. Then listen and match the speakers 1–4 to sentences A–E. There is one extra sentence.

A 'A dramatic experience changed everything and started me on this path.'

B 'I was lucky to meet people who helped and motivated me.'

C 'I've been doing it for ages, but for a long time my profession was simply a hobby.'

D 'Talent is important, but I wouldn't be here if not for my ambition and hard work.'

E 'My profession consumes me and I like it that way.'

	sentence
speaker 1	
speaker 2	
speaker 3	
speaker 4	

PREPARATION: Writing

Use the Writing Bank on page 104 to help you.

EXAM TASK – Writing

There is a competition in your school magazine and the winning entry will be published. You are invited to describe a sporting event in which you took part as a child. Write an article in 210–230 words.

In your article, you should:

- include a title
- explain what event it was
- mention your role in it
- say what happened
- explain why it was memorable

Write your article in the appropriate style and format.

PREPARATION: Speaking

Use the Functions Bank on page 102 (Giving opinions) to help you.

EXAM TASK – Speaking

Part 2 – Sustained long turn

Task 1: These two pictures show people who have achieved something. Compare and contrast them and say how you think these achievements are important to each person.

These ideas may help you:

- Situation/environment/setting
- Facial expression
- Mood
- Emotions
- Possible follow-up activities (e.g. celebration, future job/ career)
- Other

Task 2: Read the quotation below and express your opinion on it.

These ideas may help you:

- Do you agree or disagree with the quotation? Why?
- Support your opinion with an example/your own experience.

'What you get by achieving your goals is not as important as what you become by achieving your goals.' Zig Ziglar

3 From cradle to grave

A VOCABULARY
Stages of life

I can talk about the different stages of someone's life.

1 Match the stages of life in the box with a–f on the diagram. Then write the years each stage begins and ends, in your opinion.

adolescence	adulthood	childhood	infancy
middle age	old age		

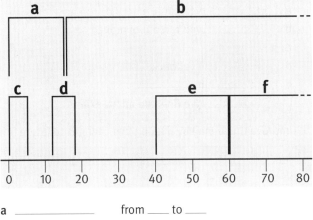

a _____ from ___ to ___
b _____ from ___ to ___
c _____ from ___ to ___
d _____ from ___ to ___
e _____ from ___ to ___
f _____ from ___ to ___

2 Solve the anagrams to make words with similar meaning.

1 a baby (an) nnifat _____
2 a young child (a) etdlord _____
3 a teenager (an) esdotcanle _____
4 children skid _____
5 old people (the) yellerd _____

3 Match the verbs in the box with the definitions.

bring up	bury	pass away	retire	settle down

1 _____ : die
2 _____ : start to have a quieter way of life
3 _____ : raise (a child)
4 _____ : stop doing your job because you have reached a certain age
5 _____ : put a dead person into a grave

● ● ● ● ● **Extension:** Phrasal verbs with *up* and *down*

4 Rewrite the sentences using a phrasal verb from the box. (sb = somebody, sth = something)

bring sb down	do sth up	hold sb up
look down on sb	own up to sth	put up with sth
put sth down to	set sth up	

1 I won't tolerate this kind of behaviour!
   I won't put up with this kind of behaviour!

2 He attributes his success to hard work.
   _____

3 He established a company to import Polish food.
   _____

4 This rain is depressing me.
   _____

5 It will cost a fortune to renovate this house.
   _____

6 He thinks he's superior to everybody!
   _____

7 I hope I'm not delaying you.
   _____

8 She confessed to having lied.
   _____

5 Complete the sentences with your own ideas.

1 I find it hard to put up with _____
   _____

2 It gets me down when people _____
   _____

3 I should cut down _____

4 This town would be a better place to live if they did up
   _____

● ● ● ● ● ● CHALLENGE! ● ● ● ● ● ●

Write six sentences about yourself at the six different stages of life from exercise 1. Use the past, present or future, as appropriate.

During infancy, _____
As a child, _____
During adolescence, _____
As an adult, _____
In middle age, _____
In old age, _____

Talking about the future

I can talk about future plans, schedules and predictions.

1 Complete the sentences with a future form of the verbs in brackets. Use each of the forms in the box once.

present continuous	present simple	will	going to

1 Hurry up! Our flight _____ (leave) in an hour!
2 I _____ (send) you a postcard, I promise.
3 We _____ (spend) a week on a boat and a week at a hotel.
4 I _____ (take) lots of photos while I'm away.

2 Complete these predictions with *will* or *going to*.

1 There's water on the floor over there. Somebody _____ slip on it.
2 The sky is so dark! It _____ rain.
3 I didn't do very well in my exams, but I'm sure I _____ do better next year.
4 I reckon I _____ get married before I'm thirty.
5 She's driving too fast. Look out! She _____ crash.

3 Write offers in response to these problems. Use your own ideas.

1 'I can't find my wallet.'
   I'll help you look for it.

2 'I'm really cold.'
   _____

3 'I don't understand this text.'
   _____

4 'I'm worried about my history exam tomorrow.'
   _____

5 'I haven't got enough money for the bus.'
   _____

6 'I've left my packed lunch at home.'
   _____

7 'I need a new outfit for a party this Saturday.'
   _____

4 Match the two halves of the sentences. Complete them with the words in the box.

as soon as	by the time	in case	unless
until	when		

1 Please wait here ☐
2 You should pay back this money ☐
3 _____ we've found the campsite, ☐
4 I'll be relieved ☐
5 _____ he asks really nicely, ☐
6 Take a credit card with you ☐

a _____ you can.
b _____ you run out of money.
c it will be dark.
d _____ I get back.
e I won't help him.
f _____ I've finished all my exams.

5 Improve this e-mail by making five changes to future forms.

> Hi Holly!
>
> How are you? Thanks for your text. I'm going to London tomorrow, but we can meet in the morning before I'll go. My train will leave at 11.45. Shall we meet at the coffee shop at 10.30? I'm not minding if you're a bit late.
>
> Pete tells me you're taking a year off before university. Are you going to spend some time abroad? Promise me you aren't going to forget about your friends back home! Maybe I'm even visiting you (if you go somewhere nice).
>
> love
> Ruth

6 Imagine you are Holly. Write an e-mail replying to Ruth. Mention your plans for next year and tomorrow's arrangement.

_____
_____
_____
_____
_____

Extra Practice

Revision: Student's Book page 29

1 Complete the colloquial phrases.

1 j_____ off to LA = flying to LA

2 p_____ it = too old

3 stuck in a r_____ = bored with the same routine

4 g_____ = man

5 like a mad t_____ = wildly

6 b_____ the drums = hitting the drums

2 Read the text. Why does an ageing population create problems for a country's economy? Tick the reasons that are mentioned.

a more houses need to be built ☐

b older people spend less money ☐

c a smaller proportion of the population is at work ☐

d taxes go up ☐

e healthcare costs are higher ☐

f they all require free games consoles ☐

3 Are these sentences true or false? Write T or F.

1 A British newspaper contained a story about elderly people playing computer games. ____

2 News stories about the care of the elderly in the UK are usually quite positive. ____

3 Most elderly people in the UK do not live with their children. ____

4 Increases in life expectancy do not necessarily lead to an ageing population. ____

5 By 2024, about a quarter of the adult population will be retired. ____

6 Three quarters of people say they would pay more tax to provide better care for the elderly. ____

●●●●●● **CHALLENGE!** ●●●●●●

Write three sentences comparing the situation described in the text with the situation in your country,

_____

_____

_____

_____

_____

_____

_____

Flossie Chambers, 89, playing ten pin bowling

When I'm 64 ...

In 2007, a British newspaper reported that elderly residents of the Sunrise Senior Living Centre were addicted to the Nintendo Wii. Apparently, the craze started when one of the chefs brought in a console that belonged to his son. Residents aged between 80 and 103 enjoyed playing the games so much that they demanded that staff buy one immediately.

However, 'good news' stories related to the care of the elderly are rare. Britain does not have a good record when it comes to caring for its elderly citizens. While in many other countries, older people often live with their children, this is much less common in the UK. Over 3.5 million older people in Britain live alone, and many do not even have regular visitors. About 500,000 people over 65 live in care homes run privately or by the state, where they may suffer from boredom, depression and even physical mistreatment.

Like most developed nations, the UK has an ageing population. This is partly because families are having fewer children, and partly because people are living longer. For the first time in our history, there are more people in the UK aged over 60 than under 16.

Of course, any increase in life expectancy is good news but there are financial consequences. In the early 1900s when pensions were first introduced, people at work outnumbered pensioners by 22 to one. It was easy for the government to pay for pensions out of taxation. However, by 2024, there will only be three people of working age for every pensioner. Inevitably, the working population will need to pay more tax to meet the pensions bill. The nation's healthcare costs are also increasing as the population grows older. About 50% of all spending on health services in the UK is for people over the age of 65.

Finding better ways of caring for an ageing population is gradually becoming a priority in the UK. A survey in 2007 revealed that 75% of British people would be prepared to pay more tax in order to improve care for the elderly (although this is not the same as actually voting for a party that plans to raise taxes). In the future, both the government and families will have to do more.

Revision: Student's Book page 30–31

1 Complete the adjectives in these sentences.

1 Something or somebody that is impossible to predict is unpredict_____.

2 Somebody who can be trusted to behave sensibly is respons_____.

3 Something which is difficult to understand is confus_____.

4 Somebody who acts in a rational, logical way is reason_____.

5 Somebody who likes to start arguments is argument_____.

6 Somebody who changes mood all the time is mood_____.

2 Complete the sentences using an appropriate tense of the phrasal verbs in the box.

come down to end up get on with grow up storm out of turn into

1 We didn't like each other at first, but we _____ being friends.

2 A large company bought the building and _____ it _____ a supermarket

3 It's difficult to _____ my work when people keep phoning me.

4 I was born in London, but I _____ in the countryside.

5 Finding a good place to live often _____ luck.

6 Sophie _____ the office when her boss accused her of stealing.

3 Read the article. Choose the best summary of the report's conclusions: a, b or c.

a The government needs to provide more money so that teenagers are less bored and more involved in their communities.

b Most teenagers are valuable members of the community, but the government needs to focus on the small minority who become involved in crime.

c There are enough recreational facilities for young people, but more money needs to be spent on dealing with the consequences of teenage crime.

4 Choose the correct answers.

1 The Youth Review was carried out by
A the Government.
B young people.
C a charity, with support from the Government.
D a charity, with support from a company.

2 According to Lily Allen, the main message from young people is
A they want more opportunities.
B they don't want to get into trouble.
C they don't need more things to do.
D they don't agree that there is a crisis.

3 What is the main cause of anti-social behaviour, according to young people?
A Boredom.
B Gangs.
C A lack of information.
D A lack of detention centres.

4 What would the Youth Centres recommended by the report offer to young people?
A Help with their problems.
B A place to meet.
C A place to learn.
D All of A–C.

5 What would be the purpose of electing Young Mayors, according to the text?
A It would help teach young people how the political system works.
B It would allow laws to be passed giving young people free public transport.
C It would give young people a voice in the community.
D It would make young people think more seriously about the issues that affect them.

5 Explain the significance of these figures from the text.

80%
The percentage of teenagers who say they have nothing to do and nowhere to go.

1 16,000

2 12%

3 62%

4 £13 billion

5 £1.6 billion

6 £35,000

Youth Review

New statistics show that, as schools in Britain prepare to break up for the holidays, over 1 million teenagers could be wandering the streets because there is nowhere else to go. The year-long enquiry consulted 16,000 UK teenagers and recommends radical action to transform their lives, including a 'youth hub' in every community to tackle anti-social behaviour and crime.

The Review, undertaken by children's charity 4Children and supported by Nestlé, comes at a time of unprecedented debate about the welfare of young people in the UK – with statistics demonstrating worrying trends in all aspects of teenagers' lives from risky behaviour to youth-on-youth violence and anti-social behaviour. Researchers spent 12 months touring each region of the country and consulting over 16,000 teenagers of all ages to find out what life is truly like for young people today in the UK and how they themselves believe that improvements can be made.

Publicising the report today, pop star and youth icon Lily Allen said: 'I want to see a new start for teenagers in communities where they have nothing to do, nowhere to go and nowhere to call their own. The Youth Review has consulted 16,000 teenagers across the country and their message was clear: they said to give young people more of a stake in communities and give us more opportunities. The number of teenagers who go off the rails is a problem for us all and instead of helping them only after they're in crisis we need to stop them getting into trouble in the first place.'

The enquiry discovered:

- Young people were fearful for their own safety, with 60% of young people in deprived areas becoming victims of crime in their community.
- 80% of young people said they had nowhere to go and nothing to do outside school and hung around on the streets as a result.
- 70% of teenagers said that, in their opinion, young people got involved in anti-social behaviour because they were bored.
- More than 70% of 11–16 year olds said that they have witnessed anti-social behaviour over the last year, whilst 12% of young people belong to a gang.
- 62% said that they did not know where to go to get help or information if they needed it.
- Youth crime costs up to £13 billion per year compared to £1.6 billion spent by the government on positive prevention and youth programmes. It costs £35,000 to put a young person in a detention centre for a year.

The Review is calling for an urgent transformation of support for teenagers. It recommends a programme of government investment and action to provide positive opportunities for all young people, with early support and intervention for troubled teenagers to prevent difficulties escalating.

The key recommendations are:

- A Youth Centre in every community providing dedicated spaces for young people to meet, as well as access to music, creative arts, sports, classes and specialist intervention and support for teenagers in difficulty.
- Mobile Intervention Teams to work in areas of high deprivation and unrest – offering teenagers specialist and positive support.
- Action on bullying and a new Victim Support scheme for young people who have been the victims of crime.
- Young Mayors elected in every area to give teenagers representation and a say in their community.
- Free public transport and leisure for all young people under 18 to ensure access for all.

Oona King, Chair of the Review said: 'Growing up can be tough and we are simply not doing enough to help the next generation to flourish. On average we spend 17p for each young person per day on youth services and this has to change. Young people need to be a part of our communities otherwise we spend billions dealing with the consequences of anti-social behaviour, crime and violence.'

●●●●●● CHALLENGE! ●●●●●●

How could the government improve the lives of young people where you live? Make three recommendations.

1 _____
_____

2 _____
_____

3 _____
_____

Future continuous and future perfect

I can talk about actions at different times in the future.

1 Look at Ricky's plan for when he finishes his education. Then complete the sentences using the future perfect simple, affirmative or negative.

2012	Get a job in an IT firm.
2013	Become a manager in the firm.
2014	Leave the firm and start a company.
2015	Sell company and retire.
2016	Move to the Caribbean.
2017	Get married.
2018	Start a family.

If everything goes according to plan for Ricky …

1 By 2015, he _____ (start / company).
2 By 2013, he _____ (leave / IT firm)
3 By 2016, he _____ (move / Caribbean)
4 By 2020, he _____ (get married)
5 By 2018, he _____ (start a family)

2 This time next month, Zoë will be on holiday. What will she be doing? Look at the pictures and write sentences in the future continuous.

This time next month …

1 <u>She'll be having dinner in a restaurant.</u>
2 _____
3 _____
4 _____
5 _____

3 Complete the sentences with the future continuous (*will be doing*) or the future perfect simple (*will have done*) of the verbs in the box.

| finish | learn | sit | tidy | wear | work |

1 Let's plan a party for next week. We _____ our exams by then.
2 The house is a mess now, but we _____ it before our parents get home.
3 What outfit do you think she _____ when she arrives?
4 I'm afraid I can't come to your wedding next month because I _____ abroad.
5 The first night of the play is next Saturday. I hope you _____ your lines by then!
6 At dinner, you _____ next to me.

4 Complete the text messages. Use the future continuous, future perfect simple or future perfect continuous of the verbs in brackets.

I ¹_____ (drive) around Spain next year. Can I come and visit you in Madrid?
REPLY   OK

I ²_____ (not live) in Madrid! I ³_____ (move) to Barcelona. But you can come and see me there. What time of year?
REPLY   OK

I ⁴_____ (arrive) in Barcelona around March, I reckon. I ⁵_____ (travel) for about six weeks by then.
REPLY   OK

OK, fine. I ⁶_____ (not live) in Barcelona for very long, so I won't know it very well.
REPLY   OK

That's OK. We can explore together. Hopefully, I ⁷_____ (learn) some Spanish by then.
REPLY   OK

Good! Although you ⁸_____ (not speak) much Spanish in Barcelona. They speak Catalan.
REPLY   OK

5 Write one sentence saying what you will have done and one saying what you will be doing in five years' time.

1 _____
_____
2 _____
_____

 Extra Practice

3F SPEAKING
Presenting arguments

I can present arguments to support my opinions effectively.

1 Choose the correct words in the useful phrases.

a I'd like to begin by **telling** / **saying** that …

b First of **everything** / **all**, …

c In my **sight** / **view**, …

d For **instance** / **instant**, …

e I don't **accept** / **allow** that.

2 Read the extract from a debate, ignoring the gaps. Match it with the proposition a, b or c.

a Your teenage years are the most difficult of your life. Do you agree? Why? / Why not?

b The Government should spend more money on providing free leisure facilities for teenagers. Do you agree? Why? / Why not?

c In today's society, teenagers have more power and influence than ever before. Do you agree? Why? / Why not?

Tom　I don't think adults really listen to teenagers' opinions. For ¹_____, governments often make changes to the education system without even asking students what they think. What's ²_____, issues which teenagers really care about, ³_____, the environment, only become important when adults start caring about them too.

Megan　I don't really ⁴_____ with that. In my ⁵_____, teenagers have a lot of different ways of saying what they think – chat rooms, for example.

Tom　But I don't ⁶_____ that anyone in authority really listens to those opinions. They don't have any effect.

3 🎧05 Complete the extract in exercise 2 with the words in the box. Then listen and check.

agree　believe　example　more　opinion　say

4 🎧06 Listen to a student debating one of the other propositions in exercise 2 with her teacher.

Which proposition is it?　_____

5 🎧06 Complete these extracts from the debate with the words in the box. Then listen again and check.

cash　generalise　independence　permission　pressure　stages

1 It's impossible to _____ about people's lives.

2 Because of the _____ of exams, many students never really get a chance to relax.

3 Teenagers often have very little _____ to spend.

4 Teenagers do not have _____.

5 If I want to go and stay with a friend, I have to ask _____ first.

6 Teenage years are more difficult than other _____ in life.

6 Imagine you are preparing to debate the other proposition from exercise 2. Decide which of these ideas support the proposition and underline them. Then add one more idea on each side of the argument.

- boredom is a cause of crime
- private gyms, etc. are expensive
- politicians don't know what teenagers enjoy
- parents should pay for their own children's leisure
- sports, etc. improve health and fitness
- free facilities help poor but talented sports people
- it's better to spend the money on education
- work experience is more use than leisure
- _____
- _____

7 Choose two ideas from exercise 6 that you agree with. Use them to make notes for your debate. Include some phrases from exercises 1 and 3.

[first idea + example] _____

_____

_____

_____

_____

[second idea + example] _____

_____

_____

_____

_____

3G WRITING
Description of a person

I can write a detailed description of a person I admire.

Preparation

1 Read the paragraphs. Which girl and boy in the photos are they describing?

JASMINE is medium height and quite slim. She's got red-brown hair which she usually has in a bob. Sometimes, when it's long enough, she has a pony tail. She's usually well-dressed and likes to wear quite trendy clothes.
I wouldn't describe her as beautiful, but she's good-looking, and she has a very attractive smile.   girl ____

ANTHONY is quite tall, with broad shoulders. He's got straight, dark hair which he usually keeps very short. In fact, at the moment, he has a crew cut! He's pale-skinned with brown eyes and quite a thin face.
He doesn't pay a lot of attention to his clothes, and often looks a bit scruffy. Once he grew a moustache, but his friends just laughed at him until he shaved it off.   boy ____

2 Match these descriptive words and phrases to the people in the photos in exercise 1. Use a dictionary if necessary.

1 skinny   _____
2 plump   _____
3 layered hair   _____
4 dark-skinned   _____
5 fair hair   _____
6 dyed fringe   _____

3 Describe yourself using words and phrases from exercises 1 and 2.

_____
_____
_____
_____

4 Match the personality adjectives on the left with words on the right with similar meaning.

artistic	patient
shrewd	hard-working
tolerant	honest
frank	sensitive
quick-tempered	creative
diligent	argumentative
emotional	clever

5 Decide which two words from exercise 4 best describe your own personality and add two more. Use them to complete the sentences.

I tend to be _____.
People often find me _____.
I have a _____ side.
I can be _____.

6 Choose somebody in your English class that you know and like. Make notes in the paragraph plan below.

1 Personal details (name, age, how long you have known them, etc):

_____

2 Appearance:

_____

3 Personality:

_____

4 What I like most about him / her :

_____

7 Use your notes from exercise 6 to write a description of your classmate. Use the writing guide below.

Writing Guide

1 Decide whether you want to include all the information from your notes.
2 Think about how to link details into longer sentences. Use the paragraphs in exercise 1 to get ideas.
3 Remember to write in paragraphs.

CHECKLIST

Have you:
- followed the paragraph plan?
- provided enough detail in the physical description?
- used appropriate phrases from exercise 4 for describing personality?
- included an example in paragraph 4?
- checked your work for mistakes?

 Extra Practice

4 Man and beast

A VOCABULARY
Animals

I can identify the different parts of an animal.

1 Label the parts of the animals.

1 _____ 6 _____ 11 _____ 16 _____
2 _____ 7 _____ 12 _____ 17 _____
3 _____ 8 _____ 13 _____
4 _____ 9 _____ 14 _____
5 _____ 10 _____ 15 _____

2 Complete the animal idioms and match them with the meanings.

1 If you are in the _____ house, ☐
2 If it is raining _____ and _____, ☐
3 If you are having a _____ of a time, ☐
4 If you let the _____ out of the bag, ☐
5 If you talk about something until the _____ come home, ☐
6 If you escape the _____ race, ☐

a you give away a secret.
b it is raining very heavily.
c you move out of the city and find a way of life that is less competitive and aggressive.
d you are really enjoying yourself.
e somebody is annoyed with you.
f you talk about it incessantly.

●●●●● **Extension: Collective nouns**

3 Put the nouns in the correct group.

bees	birds	books	cards	cows	dishes
dolphins	flowers	insects	goats	grapes	
penguins	seals	sheep	whales	wolves	

1 a flock of _____, _____
2 a herd of _____, _____
3 a bunch of _____, _____
4 a pack of _____, _____
5 a school of _____, _____
6 a swarm of _____, _____
7 a pile of _____, _____
8 a colony of _____, _____

Talking about ability

I can describe ability in the past, present and future.

1 Complete the rules with the words in the box. You will need to use some words more than once.

> be able to   being able to   can/can't   could
> couldn't   managed to do   succeeded in doing
> will be able to

1 We normally use _____ to talk about ability in the present.
2 We normally use _____ to talk about ability in the future. However, we often use _____ to talk about future arrangements.
3 We use _____ when we need an infinitive and _____ when we need an –*ing* form.
4 We only use _____ for general ability in the past. When we're talking about one occasion, we use a different expression, such as _____ or _____.
5 However, we use the negative _____ whether we are talking about general ability or one occasion.
6 We use _____ with verbs of perception, like *see*, *smell*, *hear*, *taste feel*, even if it's one occasion.

2 Choose the correct form.

1 I **can't / don't manage** to swim very well.
2 Fran **couldn't / wasn't able to** find her mobile.
3 The police **finally managed to / could finally** catch the gang of shoplifters.
4 David **didn't manage to / didn't succeed in** finish his homework on time.
5 I **could / have been able to** swim since I was six.
6 I got a pay rise last month so I **could / was able to** buy a new car.
7 We need to leave right now. **Can you / Will you be able to** take the bags out to the car?
8 Jon **didn't succeed in reading / couldn't read** very well when he was little.
9 I don't like **not being able to / not managing** drive.

3 Complete the text with *can*, *could*, *be able to*, *manage* or *succeed*. Use the correct form. Sometimes more than one answer is possible.

I ¹_____ ride since I was about six. My parents ²_____ afford to buy a horse, but there was a riding school nearby where I ³_____ learn. At first I ⁴_____ control the horse by myself but I soon learned how to make it do what I wanted. Last month I entered a show-jumping competition. Unfortunately, I ⁵_____ to win any prizes but at least I ⁶_____ finishing the course without falling off. In a few weeks we're moving to a different part of the country, but I hope ⁷_____ carry on riding, and if I'm lucky one day I might ⁸_____ have my own horse.

4 Complete the second sentence so that it has a similar meaning to the first sentence, using the word in bold.

1 Julian isn't a very good swimmer. **can**
   Julian _____ very well.
2 Do you know where I can possibly find a chemist's that is open? **able**
   Do you know where I might _____ _____ a chemist's that is open?
3 Jenny wasn't able to find a job until she moved to Manchester. **succeed**
   Jenny _____ a job until she moved to Manchester.
4 Will you manage to find the way to my house without a map? **able**
   _____ the way to my house without a map?
5 I'm much better than my brother at tennis but he succeeded in beating me yesterday. **manage**
   I'm much better than my brother at tennis but he _____ _____ me yesterday.
6 Harry couldn't find his passport so he missed his flight. **able**
   Harry missed his flight because he _____ _____ his passport.
7 How were you able to afford such an expensive television? **manage**
   How _____ such an expensive television?
8 I wasn't able to go to school yesterday as I was ill. **could**
   I was ill yesterday so I _____ _____ to school.

I can understand an article about fox hunting.

Revision: Student's Book page 39

1 Complete the sentences with the words in the box.

groom	kittens	owners	pets	put down
stuffed	treat x 2	welfare		

1 Some dog _____ take their dogs to see a pet psychologist.
2 Some people _____ their animals better than they _____ their elderly relatives.
3 Dogs and cats are the most popular _____ in the UK.
4 You can see a lot of _____ animals in the museum.
5 Our cat gave birth to five _____ last week.
6 It is advisable to _____ your dog once a week.
7 My sister works for an animal _____ charity.
8 Unfortunately our dog became very ill and we had to have it _____ .

2 Read the text quickly. Is foxhunting with dogs legal in Britain? Yes ☐ No ☐

3 Complete the text with appropriate words.

4 Are the sentences true or false? Write T or F.

1 Fox hunting started because farmers needed to kill foxes. ____
2 Foxes kill more animals than they need to survive. ____
3 Opponents of hunting argued that it wasn't necessary to kill any foxes. ____
4 There is disagreement as to whether shooting foxes is cruel or not. ____
5 Lots of people are employed in the hunting industry. ____
6 Since the ban support for hunting has decreased. ____

5 Find words that mean:

1 a type of dog often used in hunting: _____
2 chasing; running after: _____
3 an animal or insect that destroys food, plants, etc.: _____
4 an animal that kills other animals: _____
5 young sheep: _____
6 to question whether something is true: _____
7 showing kindness: _____
8 people who live in cities: _____
9 the smell that an animal leaves behind: _____

Fox hunting

Fox hunting, with packs of hounds and people on horses pursuing foxes across [1]_____ English countryside, has been around for about 300 years. It began [2]_____ a sport practised by rich land-owners, but farmers were quick to welcome fox hunting as a means of getting rid [3]_____ what they saw as a dangerous pest. Foxes in Britain have no natural predator and they kill a lot of lambs, chickens and piglets – usually far more [4]_____ they can eat. Over the centuries, fox hunting became an important part [5]_____ rural life in Britain. However, in the last few decades of [6]_____ twentieth century, opposition [7]_____ foxhunting increased, and animal welfare organisations tried to [8]_____ it banned. They didn't dispute that the fox population needed to [9]_____ controlled, but argued that hunting caused the foxes unnecessary suffering and that there were more humane methods of killing foxes, such [10]_____ shooting them. Supporters of fox hunting, [11]_____ the other hand, argued that shooting foxes is more cruel than hunting, as the animals [12]_____ rarely killed outright and often die slowly of their wounds. They also pointed [13]_____ that hunting played a vital role in rural communities and thousands of jobs depended [14]_____ it. Moreover, they claimed that opponents of hunting were mostly city-dwellers with little knowledge or understanding of the rural way of life. Nevertheless, [15]_____ government finally made hunting with hounds illegal [16]_____ 2005, a measure supported [17]_____ two-thirds of British people. Since then, many hunts have switched to 'drag hunting', in which the dogs follow a scent (on a piece of cloth that is dragged along the ground) rather than a live animal. Hunting seems [18]_____ be as popular as ever, with most hunts claiming an increase in membership. Moreover, public opinion has changed, with half of British people now believing [19]_____ the ban should be lifted.

⦿⦿⦿⦿⦿⦿ **CHALLENGE!** ⦿⦿⦿⦿⦿⦿

Should all hunting be banned? What's your opinion? Why?

_____
_____
_____
_____
_____
_____

Half human, half beast

I can talk about creatures from Greek mythology.

Revision: Student's Book page 40–41

1 Write the name of at least one animal that makes these noises.

1 bark _____
2 buzz _____
3 chatter _____
4 hiss _____
5 miaow _____
6 roar _____
7 squawk _____
8 squeak _____
9 whistle _____

2 Look at the pictures. Do you know the names of these mythical creatures? Read the text quickly and match the names to the pictures.

① ② ③ ④

3 Find twelve parts of the body in the texts and complete the chart.

Animal or human		Animal	
1 _____	2 _____	1 _____	2 _____
3 _____	4 _____	3 _____	4 _____
5 _____	6 _____		
7 _____	8 _____		

4 Read the texts. Which mythical creature:

1 was particularly dangerous for women? _____
2 lived near a city? _____
3 changes character and appearance from myth to myth? _____
4 killed itself? _____
5 lived deep under a palace? _____
6 ate people? _____
7 had the head of a woman and the body of a bird? _____
8 was particularly dangerous for travellers? _____
9 had to be imprisoned? _____
10 was used by the gods to hurt people? _____
11 represented people's basic instincts? _____
12 was killed by somebody from Athens? _____

●●●●●● **CHALLENGE!** ●●●●●●

Find out and write about another mythical creature. Think about these things:
1 Where is the myth from?
2 What did the creature look like?
3 What did it do?
4 Was it dangerous? Why?

_____
_____
_____
_____
_____
_____
_____
_____
_____
_____
_____
_____
_____
_____

Mythical creatures of Ancient Greece

A THE SPHINX

In Greek mythology, the Sphinx was a monster with the head of a woman, the body of a lion and the wings of an eagle. Its name comes from the Greek verb 'sphingo' which means 'to strangle' – which is what it did to its unfortunate victims. According to the stories, it sat on a tall rock by the road that led to Thebes, and stopped travellers on their way to and from the city. It would then ask them the following riddle: 'What walks on four legs in the morning, on two legs in the afternoon, and on three legs in the evening?' No traveller was ever able to answer the riddle, and so they were all killed by the Sphinx. Then one day, a young man called Oedipus managed to solve the riddle. When challenged by the Sphinx, he replied that a human crawls on its hands and feet as a baby, walks on two legs as an adult, and finally uses a walking stick in old age. On hearing this, the Sphinx threw itself from the rock and died, and the grateful citizens of Thebes made Oedipus their king.

B THE CENTAURS

According to Greek myths, centaurs were a tribe of creatures which were half-horse and half-human. They had the head, chest and arms of a man, and the body, tail and legs of a horse. In later myths, they also had horns and wings. Centaurs were said to live in the woods and mountains of Ancient Greece. The Greeks believed that they were savage and cruel, and a particular danger to women, who they attacked and carried off. For the Greeks, centaurs symbolised our dark, primitive natural instincts, and the battles between humans and centaurs mirrored the struggle between civilisation and barbarism. However, Chiron, the gentlest and wisest of the centaurs, was a great teacher and became tutor to Achilles, Jason and other heroes of Greek mythology. The story goes that when he died, Chiron became the constellation, Sagittarius.

C THE MINOTAUR

In Greek mythology, the Minotaur had the body of a man and the head of a bull. Pasiphae, wife of Minos King of Crete, looked after the Minotaur when it was young, but soon it became aggressive and started causing terror and destruction. At that point, Minos ordered his architect, Daedalus, to construct a gigantic labyrinth under the royal palace to hold the Minotaur. The people of Crete never saw the Minotaur again but they heard it roar and felt the ground shake as it ran around in the labyrinth. The Minotaur only ate human flesh and every year King Minos sent seven boys and girls from Athens into the tunnels of the labyrinth to face the Minotaur. They were never seen again. Then one year, Theseus, son of the King of Athens, volunteered to go into the labyrinth and kill the Minotaur. Ariadne, daughter of King Minos, gave Theseus a ball of string which he unwound as he went into the labyrinth, in order that he could find his way out again. Theseus found the Minotaur and killed it. As soon as he emerged from the labyrinth, there was a huge earthquake which destroyed the palace and buried the Minotaur's body forever.

D THE HARPIES

Harpies were first described by Homer in the *Odyssey* as beautiful fair-haired wind spirits, but in later myths they were transformed into ugly, noisy, foul-smelling birds, with insatiable appetites. They had sharp claws and wings, and the faces of ugly old women. Their name translates as 'snatchers' or 'grabbers' as they were known for snatching away people and things from the Earth. In the myths, there were three harpies and they were sisters. When they were born, they were so hideous that their parents hid them away. However, the Greek gods used them to punish people with whom they were angry. They put King Phineas on an island with the harpies. Every time he was about to eat, the harpies arrived and stole the food from his hands before he could put it into his mouth. Phineas was eventually rescued by Jason and the Argonauts, who killed one of the harpies and chased the others to the islands of the Strophades, where they remained for the rest of their lives.

4E GRAMMAR
Nominal clauses

I can recognise and use nominal clauses in written and spoken English.

1 Complete the second sentence so that it has a similar meaning to the first.

1 Keith isn't answering his phone. That's strange.
  It's strange that Keith isn't answering his phone.

2 You are here now. That's the important thing.
  The _____

3 Chelsea scored five goals. That was amazing.
  It _____

4 Philip couldn't come to my party. That was a shame.
  It _____

5 The man was seen at the scene of crime. This fact proves nothing.
  The fact _____

6 A man won the lottery on two separate occasions. That's almost beyond belief.
  It _____

2 Underline pairs of sentences in the text and rewrite them as single sentences.

Are zoos a good thing or a bad thing?

The animals are kept in unnatural conditions. This is one of the biggest criticisms of zoos. The animals are not free to roam. However, this does not mean that they suffer. Zoos are only there to attract visitors and generate profit. This is another criticism.
Zoos also do a lot of good work. That is beyond doubt. Zoos have helped to save endangered wildlife from extinction. That is one of their greatest achievements. The number of people who visit zoos and learn about animal conservation is increasing. That is encouraging.

1 The fact that animals _____

2 That the animals _____

3 Another criticism is _____

4 _____

5 _____

6 _____

3 Rewrite the sentences using *all*.

1 I just need a bit more money.
  All I need is a bit more money.

2 I just need a bit of peace and quiet.
  _____

3 I've only got £5 on me.
  _____

4 You just need to say sorry.
  _____

5 Tom just wants a good night's sleep.
  _____

6 I just need a little more time.
  _____

4 Rewrite the sentences with *what* to give more emphasis.

1 I intend to get really fit.
  What I intend to do is get really fit.

2 Ice on the road probably caused the accident.
  _____

3 Education is really important.
  _____

4 I'd really like to travel round the world.
  _____

5 Frank's laziness worries me.
  _____

6 The ending of the film surprised me.
  _____

7 I need to work faster.
  _____

 Extra Practice

4F SPEAKING
Topic presentation

I can give a presentation on a set topic with confidence.

1 Complete the phrases with prepositions from the box.

ago	at	before	for	in

1 Two centuries _____ , ...
2 _____ those days, ...
3 _____ the modern era, ...
4 _____ thousands of years, ...
5 A few decades _____ ,
6 _____ ancient societies, ...
7 _____ that time, ...

2 🎧 07 **Listen to the presentation. What is the speaker's overall opinion?**

It is wrong to keep animals in zoos. ☐
It isn't wrong to keep animals in zoos. ☐

3 🎧 07 **Listen again and complete the phrases the speaker uses.**

Introduction

1 Zoos have been a popular form of entertainment for a very _____ _____ ...
2 it is only in _____ _____ years that ...

Main part

3 My _____ _____ is that ...
4 Some people _____ that ...
5 They also _____ _____ that ...
6 There may once have been some _____ in this _____ ...
7 Nowadays, it is _____ to say that ...

Conclusion

8 So, _____ _____ _____ , I disagree that ...
9 While it's _____ that in an _____ world ...
10 I _____ believe that ...

4 Look at the exam question below and decide what your overall opinion is. Write a brief introduction that puts the question in a historical context. Use the information in the box to help you.

> Should we allow scientists to experiment on living animals in order to further scientific knowledge and to find cures for human diseases?

> First animal testing: over 2,000 years ago. Has led to a lot of medical advances.

_____
_____
_____

5 Now write the main part of your presentation. Use phrases from exercise 3 and these ideas to help you, or use your own ideas.

> **Why we should allow experiments:**
> • find cures for human diseases
> • test drugs on animals before giving to humans
> • regulations – animals in laboratories don't suffer unnecessarily
>
> **Why we shouldn't allow experiments:**
> • no right to inflict suffering on animals
> • other ways of testing drugs (e.g. computer simulations)
> • animals – same rights as humans

_____
_____
_____
_____
_____
_____
_____
_____
_____
_____

6 Write the conclusion. Sum up your ideas in one or two sentences. Use phrases from exercise 3 to help you.

_____
_____
_____

Preparation

1 Complete the text with the words in the box. Use your dictionary to help you.

appearance comprises covers course designated
endangered explore located protected size
spectacular variety varieties

The Everglades National Park

The Everglades National park is ¹_____ on the southern tip of Florida, in the USA, and ²_____ a vast wetland quite unlike any other in the world. It has been ³_____ a World Heritage Site.

The Everglades is basically a huge area of shallow, slow-moving water that ⁴_____ an enormous area – over 6,000 square kilometres. Visitors can therefore easily ⁵_____ the Everglades by boat, kayak, or canoe, but it is easy to get lost or ground the boat in shallow water, so great care needs to be taken. There is a huge ⁶_____ of plants, including the famous mangrove trees that grow out of the water and many ⁷_____ of rare orchid.

The area boasts many rare and ⁸_____ species, such as the American crocodile, Florida panther, and West Indian manatee. The Everglades are most famous for alligators, which, despite their fearsome ⁹_____ are normally wary of people. It is also possible to see ¹⁰_____ flocks of water birds feeding in the shallows and on mud flats.

The Everglades used to cover an area twice the ¹¹_____ of the present national park, but in the ¹²_____ of the twentieth century much of the original land was drained and given over to agriculture. In 1934, the area was designated a national park is now ¹³_____ from further development.

2 Make notes about a national park in your country.

Introduction
(where? most important features?) _____
_____

Landscape
(description) _____
_____

Vegetation
(plants & trees) _____
_____

Wildlife
(rare or endangered species?) _____
_____

Conservation
(why and how?) _____
_____

3 Use your notes to write a description of the national park in your country. Follow the plan below.

Writing Guide

Paragraph 1
Introduction
Paragraph 2
The landscape and vegetation
Paragraph 3
Wildlife
Paragraph 4
Conservation

CHECKLIST

Have you:
- followed the paragraph plan?
- written 200–250 words?
- checked the spelling and grammar?

 Extra Practice

EXAM TASK – Reading

Read the following article about bag snobs. Some parts of the text have been removed. Complete the text by matching the sentences (A–G) to the gaps in the text (1–6). There is one letter which you do not need to use.

My friend Julia is one of the biggest bag snobs I know. We're not talking Gucci or Chanel, although she would definitely be fussy in the high-fashion department too. ¹_____ Not for all the cash in the world would she walk down the street sporting an Asda carrier. As for Netto – she would much prefer death by 1,000 lashes in a public park than leave her house with one of those.

²_____ I regularly shop in Asda and will happily be seen with one of their carriers. I also frequent Netto, and carry the bright yellow bag with pride. My children, however, are not so comfortable with Netto bags. 'No way! I'm not taking that,' my eldest daughter protested when I handed her one of the – in my opinion fairly robust – carriers to transport cookery ingredients to school.

³_____ And there are plenty of them around. A survey has revealed us to be a nation of bag snobs, with 56 per cent of Britons believing their choice of supermarket reflects their place on the social ladder. One in eight people believe shopping at certain stores can make a person appear wealthier.

People spend on average £260 a year extra to be seen in the right shops, a survey has revealed. Many regard the supermarket they shop in as a great status symbol, with Waitrose topping the league, and cut-price stores such as Netto at the bottom. ⁴_____ Take Lidl. I was elated after my first visit – it was so cheap. The bags aren't bad-looking either.

And when surfing the web to check out what's hot and what's not in the carrier bag department (yes, such sites do exist), I came across much praise for some supermarket carriers as robust and durable. That brings me to Harrods. People seem to hang on to these bags for years. ⁵_____ But they don't care – it's the name that's important.

For some, however, no name is good enough. ⁶_____ 'I could never walk into town with my stuff in a carrier bag,' she said. I made a quick though sadly unsuccessful, attempt to hide my old Tesco bag, which contained my purse, tissues, phone and other essentials.

A A friend of mine refuses to use a carrier of any sort outside the supermarket car park.

B All I can say is that people must be crazy to miss out on the fantastic bargains to be had in cut-price stores.

C I recently mentioned to my bag snob friend how much I disliked some supermarket carrier bags.

D I am referring to carrier bags – the plastic ones we use at the checkout.

E Through no fault of mine, she is well on her way to becoming what is commonly known as a 'bag snob'.

F They are so reluctant to part with this scrap of plastic that it becomes a crumpled mess.

G I'm the complete opposite.

EXAM TASK – Use of English

Complete the text with suitable words. Use one word only in each gap.

Everyone can have a bad day. The bus is late, your computer goes on the blink and the coffee machine has ¹_____ down again. But what happens when every day is a bad ²_____ and your frustration is escalating ³_____ of control? According to psychologists, anger is ⁴_____ increasingly common problem nowadays. Calls to round-the-clock helplines ⁵_____ risen significantly over the past year – not ⁶_____ from those feeling simmering resentment but also those suffering abuse from an angry colleague. So ⁷_____ can you control the rage? Think about exactly who you are angry at and write down possible solutions. Recognise the things that you cannot change and accept ⁸_____ . Relaxation techniques, like exercise or meditation, also ⁹_____ in handy. Finally, ¹⁰_____ of being frustrated, try to look at the positive side and be happy about the good things in your life.

EXAM TASK – Listening

🎧08 **You will hear part of a radio programme about life in a monastery in Thailand. Read sentences 1–10. Then complete the sentences 1–10 with one word according to the information you hear.**

1 The first animal was brought to the monastery by the _____ .

2 Later they also gave unwanted _____ to the monks.

3 In the winter of 1999 they had the first _____ in the monastery.

4 Before it appeared there, its owner wanted to have it _____ .

5 In July 1999 this animal _____ .

6 The areas surrounding the monastery entice many _____ .

7 One animal is worth up to _____ .

8 When they started looking after the animals, the monks had had no _____ in how to treat them.

9 The monastery has changed into a(n) _____ .

10 The monks are constructing a(n) _____ for some of the animals.

PREPARATION: Writing
Use the Writing Bank on page 107 to help you.

EXAM TASK – Writing

You have just returned from holiday in Greece. During the return flight, one of your suitcases got lost and *Floria Airlines* hasn't found it so far. Write a letter of 100–120 words to the airline company.

In your letter:
- say why you are writing
- describe what you have lost
- request the quick return of your luggage
- suggest a possible solution if it is not found

Write your letter in the appropriate style and format.

PREPARATION: Speaking
Use the Functions Bank on page 102 to help you.

EXAM TASK – Speaking

Part 4 – Role play
Work in pairs and role-play the following situation.

Role A – You are B's son/daughter. It is your 18th birthday in two weeks and you want to give a party to which you would like to invite your friends and schoolmates. Discuss it with your parent, B, and ask him/her for help with preparations.

Role B – You are A's parent. It is his/her 18th birthday in two weeks and s/he wants to give a party. You are not going to be at home then and so want to discuss the 'party house rules'. You are willing to help with the preparations.

You may use these ideas:
- kind of party (costume?)
- what to prepare
- party 'house rules'
- who does what (shopping, invitations, decorations, etc.)

Role B starts the conversation. When you have finished, change your roles and practise again.

5 In the news

A VOCABULARY
Headlines

I can understand the language of newspaper headlines.

1 Look at the photo. Choose the best headline for this news story.

a Pre-Christmas surge boosts retail profits

b Blaze at shop sparks police probe

c Shop chief to quit as 1000 jobs axed

2 Match the headline words (1–16) with the words in the box.

> argument / fight   attempt   be about to happen
> cause / set off   cut   get married   increase (v.)
> investigation   manager / head   most important
> mystery   police officer   promise   request (n)
> resign   support (v.)

1 loom (v.) _____
2 pledge _____
3 bid _____
4 quit _____
5 boost (v.) _____
6 back (v.) _____
7 clash _____
8 axe (v.) _____

9 cop _____
10 riddle _____
11 top (adj.) _____
12 plea (n.) _____
13 probe (n.) _____
14 chief _____
15 spark (v.) _____
16 wed _____

3 Complete the headlines with words from exercise 2. Then write a complete sentence explaining each headline.

1
> Voters _____ green campaign

_____
_____

2
> 1500 jobs to be _____ d at car factory

_____
_____

3
> PM _____s to boost Education spending

_____

4
> Deadline _____s in CO$_2$ talks

_____
_____

5
> TV chief to _____ after corruption scandal

_____
_____

6
> Police in _____ for witnesses

_____
_____

7
> Cop hero dies in _____ with terrorists

_____
_____

8
> Fuel price surge _____s riots

_____
_____

9
> Soap stars to _____ on Caribbean beach

_____
_____

> ●●●●●● **CHALLENGE!** ●●●●●●
>
> Find some interesting headlines on British newspaper websites (e.g. www.mirror.co.uk). Write them here along with explanations.
>
> 1 _____
> _____
> _____
> 2 _____
> _____
> _____
> 3 _____
> _____
> _____

1 Change the direct speech to reported speech.

1 'I hate reading newspapers.'
Toby says _____

2 'I'd like to listen to the news on the radio.'
Sue said _____

3 'You haven't been listening to me.'
Sam complained _____

4 'I'll be working at home tomorrow.'
My dad said _____

5 'You shouldn't be so sensitive.'
Chris says _____

6 'I hadn't expected Tom to arrive so soon.'
Jeff explained _____

2 Read the dialogue and complete Mandy's report of the conversation.

Mandy What are you doing?
Kevin I'm writing a letter to the newspaper
Mandy What's the letter about?
Kevin It's about crime rates in our town. There should be more police!
Mandy You should mention that recent bank robbery.
Kevin I will, if I can find the name of the bank.
Mandy Have you looked online?
Kevin I can't. Somebody has stolen my laptop!

I asked Kevin what _____.
He explained that _____.
I asked _____, and Kevin replied
_____. He said that _____
_____. I said _____
_____ and Kevin said _____ if. I asked _____
_____. He said _____
because _____!

3 Imagine you are a journalist preparing an article about a bank robbery. Report the questions you asked one of the members of staff.

1 How long have you worked at the bank?
I asked him _____

2 What is your job title?
I asked him _____

3 Did you see the robbery?
I asked him _____

4 How much money did the robbers steal?
I asked him _____

5 Was it a frightening experience?
I asked him _____

6 Is it the first robbery at the bank?
I asked him _____

4 Match the answers (a–f) with the questions in exercise 3.

a I'm not sure, but probably £20,000 or more. ☐
b I'm the assistant manager. ☐
c Yes, I did. I was serving a customer. ☐
d No. It happened four years ago. ☐
e For six years. ☐
f Yes, it was, but everybody stayed calm. ☐

5 Now complete your article.

Yesterday, there was a robbery at the ABC Bank in the High Street. I spoke to Sam Wilson, the assistant manager, who told me that he [1]_____ at the time of the robbery. He wasn't sure exactly [2]_____ _____ but estimated that [3]_____ _____ or more. He said that [4]_____ experience but he insisted that everyone [5]_____ _____. Mr Wilson informed me that another robbery [6]_____ _____ at the same bank.

Extra Practice

Revision: Student's Book page 51

1 Complete the definitions with words from the box.

> circulation   dailies   gossip column
> quality newspaper   tabloid

1 The number of copies that a newspaper regularly sells is called its _____ .

2 A regular article in a newspaper about the private lives of famous people is called a _____ .

3 Newspapers which are published Monday to Saturday are called _____ .

4 A newspaper which contains little serious analysis is called a _____ .

5 A newspaper which contains a lot of serious analysis is called a _____ .

2 Complete the text. Use the words given to form new words that fit the gaps.

3 Choose the correct answers.

1 In 1500, Wynkin de Worde started…

   A the first printing shop in Fleet Street.

   B the first daily newspaper in England.

   C the first weekly pamphlet in London.

2 Fleet Street was ideally situated for gathering what kinds of news stories?

   A Royal, political and cultural.

   B Business, political and crime.

   C International, crime and sports.

3 Why did the newspapers pay for the journalists' food and drink?

   A The journalists did not earn high salaries.

   B The bars and restaurants were owned by the newspapers.

   C The long meals were part of the journalists' work.

4 Since the 1980s, Fleet Street has lost its unique atmosphere mainly because

   A the journalists started using mobile phones.

   B the newspapers have moved their offices to other parts of London.

   C many journalists have been replaced by computers.

5 Peter McKay compares journalists today with battery hens because

   A they earn so little money.

   B they are not very popular with the general public.

   C they work alone, as if they were in cages.

FLEET STREET

Fleet Street is a street in the centre of London, [1] _____named_____ (name) after the Fleet River which used to run nearby. It is also synonymous with the [2] _____ (England) press because of its [3] _____ (history) links with newspapers.

The first printer in Fleet Street was called Wynkin de Worde, and opened his shop in 1500. Soon, the area became well known for the printing of books and pamphlets and during the 1700s, the first [4] _____ (day) newspapers appeared. By the middle of the 20th century, almost every major newspaper in England had its head office in Fleet Street. It was the perfect [5] _____ (locate) for gathering news: close to the City, the [6] _____ (finance) centre of London; the Old Bailey, which is the main [7] _____ (crime) court, and the Palace of Westminster (the British parliament). There were also plenty of pubs and restaurants on Fleet Street where journalists would spend hours interviewing their 'contacts' while enjoying large quantities of [8] _____ (expense) food and drink which their employers paid for!

During the 1980s, it became clear that technology was changing the way newspapers were produced and that new premises were needed. *The Times* and *The Sun*, both owned by Rupert Murdoch, were the first to move away from [9] _____ (centre) London to the eastern edge of the capital. Gradually, all the other papers followed. Printing became [10] _____ (computer). Journalists began spending more time on their mobile phones and less time on their [11] _____ (prolong) business lunches. But many older journalists are still unhappy about the changes. One of them, a gossip columnist called Peter McKay, wrote in *The Independent* in 2005: 'Fleet Street was a seething mass of printers, advertisers and journalists, drinking and punching each other every night, all night. People [12] _____ (literal) never went home: there was a Turkish bath we went to for a shave in the morning … Nowadays we sit in the far corners of London, like battery hens at computer terminals, pecking out our stuff and never meeting one another.'

I can understand an article about a photo-journalist.

Revision: Student's Book page 52–53

1 Complete the text with words from the box.

> invite   misery   obsession   paparazzi
> privacy   public eye   publicity-hungry   pursue
> responsible

Do we have an unhealthy [1]_____ with the private lives of famous people? Many celebrities claim that the journalists and [2]_____ who [3]_____ them make their lives a [4]_____ . They say that they have a right to [5]_____ . However, many people argue that [6]_____ celebrities are themselves [7]_____ for this state of affairs. They benefit from being in the [8]_____ and often actively [9]_____ attention from the press.

2 Read the first two paragraphs of the text. Explain in your own words the difference between a photo-journalist and a member of the paparazzi.

_____
_____
_____
_____

3 Are the sentences true or false? Write T or F. For each statement write the letter of the paragraph where you find the evidence for your decision.

1 Photo-journalists are no less ruthless than paparazzi. ____ ____

2 Margaret Bourke-White's father was born in The Bronx in New York. ____ ____

3 When Margaret was growing up, it was not common for women to study at university. ____ ____

4 When Margaret was an industrial photographer, she was surrounded by men who refused to accept that a woman could do her job. ____ ____

5 During the 1930s, her most famous photographs showed people enjoying the 'American dream'. ____ ____

6 She published a book containing images of the Great Depression. ____ ____

7 Margaret spent a lot of time in dangerous situations during her career. ____ ____

8 Her impatience to get a good photo was one of the keys to her success. ____ ____

4 Read the text again and answer the questions.

1 Why are some news photographers called photo-journalists?
_____

2 How can a picture change government policy?
_____

3 In what two ways did Joseph White influence his daughter's future?
_____

4 How did Margaret Bourke-White gain the respect of her peers?
_____

5 What economic event from American history did Bourke-White record?
_____

6 What was Bourke-White allowed to do that women had not done before?
_____

7 What important talent did Bourke-White possess?
_____

5 Match the highlighted verbs in the text with these definitions.

1 recorded the details of _____
2 forced _____
3 was a perfect example of _____
4 left somewhere you can't get away from _____
5 made sure _____
6 hit by an underwater bomb _____
7 received from an older relative _____

●●●●●● **CHALLENGE!** ●●●●●●

Imagine you are a photo-journalist. Think of three things you want to take a photograph of in order to bring them to the public's attention.

1 _____
2 _____
3 _____

Pictures that tell a story

A Press photographers are often criticised for the way they chase after celebrities, robbing them of their privacy and sometimes even putting them at risk of physical injury. They have the reputation of being ruthless and insensitive: they will do anything they need to do in order to get an embarrassing or revealing photo of a famous person.

B However, not all press photographers can be labelled paparazzi. There is a long tradition of photographers who use their skill to show the truth about current events and to bring important issues to the attention of the public. These photographers are called photo-journalists, because their pictures tell a story. They may be just as ruthless as the paparazzi in their attempts to get the right shot, but their aim is not primarily to make money – it is to make sense of the world. Some of the most famous photo-journalists in history have been particularly interested in showing the injustices that are often hidden from the public's view. On a few occasions, a single photo has changed public opinion and compelled governments to act in a different way.

C Margaret Bourke-White was born in 1904 in The Bronx, a suburb of New York City. Her father, Joseph White, who originally came from Poland, worked in the printing industry as an engineer. Unusually for that time, he believed that girls and boys should receive an equal education, and ensured that his daughter Margaret continued her education through school and university. He was also a keen amateur photographer and Margaret inherited his love of cameras.

Chrysler Building, New York, 1931

D In the 1920s, Margaret became the first woman to be employed as a photo-journalist. She photographed major industrial and construction projects: steel factories, bridges, dams and skyscrapers. It was a man's world, but Margaret earned respect wherever she went because of her intelligence, her personality and above all, the quality of her pictures.

E In the 1930s, she documented the suffering of poor people during the Great Depression and published them in a book called *You Have Seen Their Faces*. It was a classic work of photo-journalism which epitomised the problems of American society at that time. One of her most famous pictures from that decade shows a line of poor black Americans queuing for food in front of a poster advertising the American way of life. The message is clear: 'Look at the difference between the dream and the reality!'

Bread Line during the Louisville flood, Kentucky. 1937

F Her career as a photo-journalist brought excitement and danger. She was the first female photographer to be allowed into combat zones during World War II. During her working life, she was on a boat that was torpedoed in the Mediterranean, she was stranded on an Arctic island, she was in Moscow during bombing raids, and she was rescued from a river after her helicopter crashed.

G Technically, Margaret Bourke-White was a skilful and innovative photographer. She also had the personal qualities that are necessary for a successful photo-journalist, such as bravery, perseverance and patience. But perhaps most importantly, she had the gift of knowing where the next big news story was going to happen. She somehow always managed to be in the right place at the right time.

GRAMMAR
Reporting verbs

I can report what people have said in a variety of ways.

1 Change the sentences into reported speech. Use the reporting verbs in the box and a *that* clause.

admit	announce	~~complain~~	explain	promise

1 'It's not fair!'
   He complained that it wasn't fair.
2 'It was my fault.'
   I _____
3 'I won't stay out late tonight.'
   She _____
4 'I went to bed early because I was feeling tired.'
   I _____
5 'I'm going to take early retirement.'
   He _____

2 Write the words in the correct order. Then match three of the sentences with the pictures. Write the numbers in the speech bubbles.

1 you / to / the / I / near / not / sit / edge / warned
   _____

2 I / me / another / that / tell / insisted / should / she / joke
   _____

3 I / now / this / T-shirt / against / understand / why / advised / you / me / wearing
   _____
   _____

4 I / messy / being / can't / you / of / accuse / well
   _____

5 admit / she / your / doesn't / him / number / giving / to
   _____

3 Complete the sentences with a preposition if necessary and the infinitive or *–ing* form of the verbs in the box.

get	give	help	pay	revise	steal	swim	use

1 The police accused him _____ Toby's mobile.
2 Tania offered _____ me a lift to the station.
3 I congratulated Daniel _____ a new job.
4 Fred agreed _____ me with the housework.
5 Harry's dad encouraged him _____ well before the exam.
6 My dad forbade me _____ his computer.
7 The lifeguard warned us not _____ from that particular beach.
8 Joanna insisted _____ for the meal, even though she was short of money.

4 Complete sentence b so that it has a similar meaning to sentence a. Use the word in bold.

1 a 'You must come home before midnight,' said Mr Jones to his son. **insisted**
   b Mr Jones insisted that his son should come home before midnight.
2 a 'I'm not going to buy you a new DVD player,' said Kate. **refused**
   b Kate _____ her a new DVD player.
3 a 'I think you should apply for a place at university, ' my dad said to me. **encouraged**
   b My dad _____ for a place at university.
4 a 'Why don't we go out for a meal,' said Fred. **suggested**
   b Fred _____ for a meal.
5 a 'I'm really sorry I broke the vase,' said Millie. **apologised**
   b Millie _____ the vase.
6 a 'Eat fruit every day,' Dr Jones said to her. **recommended**
   b Dr Jones _____ fruit every day.
7 a 'Well done for passing your driving test,' said my dad to me. **congratulate**
   b My dad _____ my driving test.

Talking about statistics

I can interpret graphs and tables, and describe trends.

1 🎧 09 Listen and write down the decimals, fractions and percentages that you hear.

1 _____   6 _____

2 _____   7 _____

3 _____   8 _____

4 _____   9 _____

5 _____   10 _____

2 Match the fractions with their equivalents.

1 half = _____

2 a quarter = _____

3 nine tenths = _____

4 a fifth = _____

5 three quarters = _____

6 a third = _____

a 25%
b One in three.
c 20%
d 0.5
e Nine out of ten.
f 0.75

3 Write these numbers and fractions as words.

1 ¼ = _a quarter_

2 ⁴/₅ = _____

3 ¹/₁₀ = _____

4 ²/₃ = _____

5 1 ¾ = _____

6 2 ½ = _____

4 Look at the sales charts. Which chart shows sales:

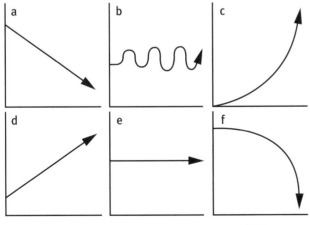

1 fluctuating? ☐   4 falling sharply? ☐
2 staying the same? ☐   5 rising sharply? ☐
3 rising steadily? ☐   6 falling steadily? ☐

5 🎧 10 Listen to the manager of a language school talking about the number of students attending classes. Draw a graph that matches the statistics.

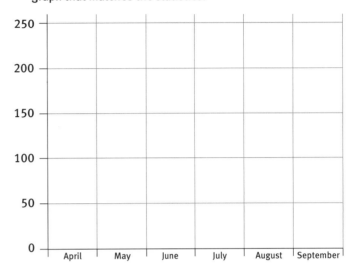

6 Complete the sentences about the statistics in the chart.

How do people get to work?		
	2000	2008
Car	49%	46%
Bus	27%	25%
Train	19%	19%
Bicycle	3%	7%
On foot	2%	3%

1 In 2008, 2% fewer people _____ _____ than in 2000.

2 Between 2000 and 2008, _____ _____ by 50%.

3 Between 2000 and 2008, _____ _____ more than doubled.

4 There was no change in _____ _____

5 _____ _____ by 3%.

6 A quarter of the people _____ _____

Preparation

My favourite TV show of all time is *Friends*. It's an American sitcom about a group of friends who live in New York. It was [1]_____ broadcast between 1994 and 2004, but it is still often shown on TV.

The story is mainly [2]_____ in the coffee shop below the apartment block where most of the characters live, and it [3]_____ the frequently complicated lives of the six friends. There are three guys and three girls, all with clearly defined [4]_____. In the early series of the show, Monica and Rachel share an apartment. Monica is the bossy, organised [5]_____, while Rachel is fashion-conscious and a [6]_____ spoiled. Phoebe is a bit of a hippy and rather strange. Across the hall from the girls' apartment is where Joey and Chandler live. Joey gets all the girls, and Chandler gets none! Chandler is the group's [7]_____, although everyone is really funny. The final [8]_____ is Ross, Monica's brother, who is a professor of palaeontology. The [9]_____ I like *Friends* so much is that it always makes me laugh. The script is really clever, the storylines are great and every episode is packed with hilarious jokes. [10]_____, the cast is really strong, although my absolute [11]_____ character has to be weird and wonderful Phoebe. However, they are all [12]_____ and they interact really well together. In [13]_____, it's a clever sitcom that hasn't dated at all. I can watch the episodes again and again and still find them funny. I would [14]_____ this to anyone who needs cheering up.

1 Complete the review with the words and phrases in the box.

> character   comedian   favourite   follows
> furthermore   little   memorable   originally   one
> personalities   reason   recommend   set   short

2 Find the words in the box in the review and match them with the definitions (1–8).

> of all time   be broadcast   script   packed with
> cast   date (v)   episode   storyline

1 all the actors in a film, play, etc. _____
2 a single TV show that is part of a series _____
3 to become old-fashioned and out of date _____
4 ever _____
5 full of _____
6 the written text of a TV programme or play _____
7 be shown on TV _____
8 plot _____

3 Write a review of a TV sitcom or drama series that you really like. Follow the plan.

Writing Guide

Paragraph 1
- name of the programme, type of programme, background information

Paragraph 2
- the story and the characters

Paragraph 3
- what you like about it

Paragraph 4
- overall opinion and recommendation

> ### CHECKLIST
>
> **Have you:**
> - followed the paragraph plan?
> - used the present simple to talk about the characters and the story?
> - counted the words and added or removed details to adjust the length?
> - checked the spelling and grammar?

Extra Practice

6 Points of view

A VOCABULARY
Opinion and belief

I can use the language of opinions and beliefs.

1 Read the sentences and complete the puzzle.

1 I don't _____ that global warming is caused only by human activity. I think there are other factors too.

2 _____ it! You made a mistake.

3 He didn't exactly say so, but he _____ strongly that I had misled him.

4 It is _____ that the plane crashed in the jungle, but nobody knows for sure.

5 Try to _____ the meaning of the word from the context.

6 I _____ that we'll find life on other planets in the solar system.

7 I _____ whether Harry knows he's got his jumper on back to front.

8 I _____ that you borrow my phone. It's no trouble.

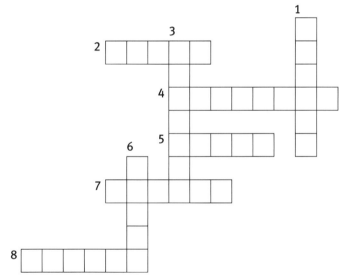

2 Rewrite the sentences using the words given.

1 I am absolutely sure that Tom is lying. (convinced)

_____

2 I don't think the present government will win the election. (doubt)

_____

3 Samantha said that she had not hit her little brother. (deny)

_____

4 Jason made me feel certain that I was wrong. (persuade)

_____

5 David doesn't accept the idea that money is more important than friendship. (reject)

_____

6 Kate reluctantly accepted that the accident was her fault. (admit)

_____

7 Harry became aware that Joe wasn't listening to him. (realise)

_____

8 The police asked the witness lots of questions about what she had seen. (quiz)

_____

●●●●● Extension: Expressing opinions

3 Choose the correct preposition.

1 She managed to persuade the police **about** / **of** her innocence.

2 Do you believe **in** / **about** God?

3 What do you think **about** / **over** nuclear power?

4 Are you **in** / **on** favour **of** / **to** capital punishment?

5 Chris has strong views **on** / **over** marriage and divorce.

6 I'm not convinced **of** / **to** the government's ability to avoid a recession.

7 I don't have any doubts **on** / **about** Jamie's schoolwork. He's doing very well.

8 **In** / **On** my view, there should be a complete ban on smoking.

9 **To** / **In** my mind, hunting is wrong.

10 I don't go along **to** / **with** the view that we should ban advertising on TV.

6B GRAMMAR
Question forms

I can write indirect questions.

1 Write subject or object questions.

1 Something is moving in that tree.
   What's moving in that tree?

2 One of the girls started crying.
   Which girl started crying?

3 James met somebody in town.
   _____

4 Somebody came into the room.
   _____

5 Celia gave him something to read.
   _____

6 Something is missing from the drawer.
   _____

7 I'd like one of those sandwiches.
   _____

8 Henry has got something in his pocket.
   _____

9 Somebody fell off their chair.
   _____

10 Sarah ran over something in her car.
   _____

2 Put the words in the correct order to make indirect questions about the photo.

1 is / any / it / Have / what / you / idea / ?
   _____

2 where / know / came / you / it / from / Do / ?
   _____

3 it's / an / know / if / really / alien spacecraft / like to / I'd / .
   _____

4 photo / you / tell / the / Could / who / took / me / ?
   _____

5 genuine / wonder / is / the / I / if / photo / .
   _____

3 Rewrite the questions, making them less formal.

1 With whom did you discuss your plans?
   _____

2 Whom did you meet at the party?
   _____

3 To whom did Tom give the money?
   _____

4 With whom did you stay?
   _____

5 To whom did you speak?
   _____

4 Write indirect questions. Use each of the phrases in the box once.

I wonder …	I'd like to know …
Could you tell me …?	Can you tell me …?
Have you any idea …?	Do you know …?
Would you mind telling me …?	

1 Where do you live?
   _____

2 What time do you plan to leave?
   _____

3 When does the next train from Brighton arrive?
   _____

4 What happened?
   _____

5 Would you be willing to donate some money to charity?
   _____

6 Why are you smiling?
   _____

7 Will you need a taxi?
   _____

 Extra Practice

Revision: Student's Book page 61

1 Complete the chart.

religion	adjective	follower	place of worship
1 _____	Buddhist	2 _____	temple
3 _____	Christian	4 _____	church
5 _____	Hindu	6 _____	temple
7 _____	Islamic	8 _____	mosque
9 _____	Jewish	10 _____	synagogue
11 _____	Sikh	12 _____	gurdwara

2 Complete the text with appropriate words.

THE CHURCH OF ENGLAND

Christianity arrived in Britain ¹_____ the first or second centuries, probably via Ireland and Spain, but it only became firmly established when the Pope sent St Augustine from Rome in the sixth century ²_____ convert the people of Britain, especially the newly arrived Saxons, to Christianity. ³_____ the help of Christians already living in Kent, Augustine established his church in Canterbury and became ⁴_____ first in the series of Archbishops of Canterbury, unbroken to this day.

For the next 1,000 years, England was part ⁵_____ the Roman Catholic Church. But in 1534, during the reign of King Henry VIII, the English church separated from Rome. The principle reason ⁶_____ the split was that Henry VIII wanted to divorce his wife, Catherine of Aragon. Pope Clement VII refused to agree ⁷_____ Henry's request and so Henry decided to become head of the Church of England himself ⁸_____ order to ensure that the divorce went through and that he could marry the second of his six wives.

England briefly rejoined ⁹_____ Roman Catholic Church during the reign of Queen Mary in 1555, but reverted to protestantism after her sister Elizabeth I came to the throne. In the seventeenth century there was conflict ¹⁰_____ the Puritans, who wanted further reform, and the church, ¹¹_____ wanted to retain traditional beliefs and practices.

3 Are the sentences true or false? Write T or F.

1 St Augustine came to Britain via Ireland and Spain. ____
2 Augustine was the first to introduce Christianity to Britain. ____
3 Some Christians who already lived in Britain helped Augustine to set up his church. ____
4 England remained in the Catholic Church until the sixteenth century. ____
5 King Henry VIII broke away from the Catholic Church because the Pope wouldn't do what he wanted. ____
6 Catherine of Aragon was Henry's second wife. ____
7 England briefly became a Catholic country again when Elizabeth became queen. ____
8 There was a struggle between the church and the Puritans. ____
9 King Charles I was on the side of the Puritans. ____
10 Catholics were discriminated against for many years following the Restoration of the monarchy. ____
11 The heir to the British throne can marry whoever he or she likes. ____

This led ¹²_____ a bloody civil war in which King Charles I was executed ¹³_____ the Puritans. However, the monarchy and the Church of England were restored in 1660, and to this day, the British monarch is still the head of the Church of England. For many decades following the Restoration of 1660, Catholics were excluded from public life and could not ¹⁴_____ elected to Parliament, but gradually they were granted full rights and liberties. However, the heir to the British throne ¹⁵_____ still forbidden by law to marry a Catholic.

I can understand an article about TV scandals.

Revision: Student's Book page 62–63

1 Complete the sentences with the correct form of the verbs in the box. Use some of the verbs twice.

admit   appear   argue   decline   find   maintain

1 The doorman refused to _____ the teenagers into the nightclub.
2 Despite being _____ guilty by the court the man still _____ his innocence.
3 Have you ever _____ on TV?
4 Harriet _____ my offer of a lift, saying she preferred to walk.
5 It costs a lot of money to _____ such a large house and garden.
6 Why can't you just _____ that you are wrong?
7 My little brother and sister are always _____ with each other.
8 The ratings for TV quiz shows have _____ in recent years.
9 Do you think that scientists will one day _____ a cure for cancer?
10 It _____ that the contestant had been cheating.
11 The students _____ for a day's holiday before the exams, but the teachers rejected the idea.

2 Read the text quickly. How many of the programmes actually admitted deceiving the viewers? _____

3 For questions 1–12, choose the correct TV programme: A, B, C or D.

Which TV programme:
1 showed a sequence of events in the wrong order? ☐
2 is particularly popular with children? ☐
3 made a lot of money from the viewers? ☐
4 was about the daily life of somebody well known? ☐
5 invited viewers to enter competitions? ☐
6 invited viewers to name a pet animal? ☐
7 implied that the presenter did something which in fact he didn't do? ☐
8 is broadcast in the morning? ☐
9 showed somebody getting angry? ☐
10 had to pay a large fine? ☐
11 showed people how to cook food? ☐
12 deceived the viewers on two separate occasions? ☐

4 Are the sentences true or false? Write T or F.

1 In 2007 the British public were deceived by TV companies. _____
2 Two programmes cheated their viewers in competitions. _____
3 All of the programmes showed events that weren't true. _____
4 Only one of the scandals lead to the TV company paying a fine. _____
5 None of the shows were cancelled as a result of the scandals. _____
6 Two of the shows apologised to their viewers. _____
7 All the people involved in the scandals lost their jobs. _____

5 Match the highlighted words in the text with these definitions.

1 to arrange a result dishonestly in advance _____
2 people who watch TV _____
3 well known for being bad _____
4 become known _____
5 going out quickly and angrily _____
6 a series of scenes from a TV programme or film shown in advance to advertise it _____
7 said sorry _____
8 give money back _____
9 made to appear real when it in fact isn't _____
10 got money illegally by tricking somebody _____

●●●●●● **CHALLENGE!** ●●●●●●
Do you ever take part in TV phone-ins? Why? / Why not?
_____
_____
_____
_____
_____
_____

It must be true – I saw it on TV

In 2007 there was a string of scandals in which TV programmes rigged phone-in competitions or misled viewers in other ways. The extensive press coverage led to a loss of confidence in the TV companies, which were perceived by the public as greedy and dishonest. Here are four of the most notorious cases …

A Blue Peter

Blue Peter is one of the UK's most famous and popular children's TV programmes – it is also the longest-running. In January last year viewers were invited to visit the programme's website and choose a name for a pet kitten that appeared on the show. Thousands of children took part in the poll and the most popular name turned out to be Cookie. However, the programme-makers ignored the voters' wishes and named the cat Socks instead, allegedly because they were worried that the name Cookie would encourage childhood obesity. When the deception came to light the editor of the programme was sacked. The presenters made a humble apology on air, and Socks was joined by a second kitten – this time called Cookie. It wasn't the first time the programme had deceived its viewers. A few months prior to the kitten-naming scandal, the presenters had faked the winner of a phone-in competition.

B A year with the Queen

In October Peter Fincham, the head of the TV channel BBC 1, was forced to resign after a scandal caused by a trailer for a documentary which misrepresented the Queen. The documentary follows the life of the Queen and other members of the royal family over a period of months as they carry out their daily duties. At the documentary's press launch, Peter Fincham told journalists that in the programme the monarch would be shown angrily storming out of a photoshoot with the renowned American photographer Annie Leibovitz. However, the footage of her supposedly stormy exit (after Miss Leibovitz asked her to remove her tiara) was in fact filmed as she arrived for the session, and had then been edited to make it look as if she got angry during the interview. It was also later revealed that Mr Fincham knew on the day of the press launch that the trailer was misleading, but didn't tell anybody.

The BBC apologised to the Queen but she was said still to be 'extremely angry' about being misrepresented in the trailer. However, she made no objection to the screening of the documentary and it was broadcast just before Christmas.

C GMTV

An investigation by the TV industry regulator has revealed that GMTV ('Good Morning Television') defrauded viewers out of about £40 million. Over a four year period, viewers were invited to take part in phone-in quizzes using premium-rate phone lines. What the participants didn't realise, however, was that the winners were determined before the phone lines closed. Between January 2003 and March 2007, over a third of the calls received were not entered into the competitions. 25 million viewers therefore each spent up to £1.80 on calls which gave them absolutely no chance of winning the competition. Over this period, GMTV made nearly £50 million in profit from its phone-ins. The company admitted full responsibility, was fined £2 million and offered to refund viewers. However, the head of the company refused to sack any of the employees responsible for the deception.

D Celebrity Chef

Celebrity chef Gordon Ramsay was accused of deceiving viewers on his highly popular cookery programme. Channel 4, the TV channel that broadcasts the programme, admitted that a scene which appeared to show Ramsay catching fish off the south coast of Britain had in fact been faked. The celebrity chef was seen on-screen diving into the water, armed with a spear-gun. He was then shown returning to the beach holding several large fish which he seemed to have caught. However, although Ramsay did in fact take part in the fishing expedition, he failed to spear any fish. It was revealed that a spear-fishing expert, Dave O'Callaghan, had in fact caught the fish which Ramsay then barbecued on the beach. Channel 4 apologised to viewers and blamed the independent television company that had made the programme for misrepresenting the true facts.

'It's my turn, isn't it?'

1 Match the question tags in the box with the sentences.

> can't he? did he? doesn't he? has he? wasn't he?
> won't he?

1 Harry was driving too fast, _____

2 This time tomorrow John will be arriving in New York,

_____

3 Fred said nothing stupid, _____

4 John can swim, _____

5 Peter lives in Liverpool, _____

6 Steve hasn't been to the States, _____

2 Complete the sentences with question tags.

1 You don't like bananas, _____

2 Don't be late, _____

3 There isn't any bread, _____

4 Kate and George had to go to London, _____

5 Everyone loves cartoons, _____

6 I didn't step on your toe, _____

7 Nothing really happens in the film, _____

8 We must leave now, _____

9 You never help with the housework, _____

10 You won't mind if I bring my sister to the party,

_____

11 Let's get a take-away, _____

12 Everything in the garden looks beautiful, _____

13 You hadn't realised I was here, _____

14 Nobody wants to go out, _____

15 Pass me the dictionary, _____

16 Do help yourself to more coffee, _____

3 Add question tags to the dialogue.

Mum   Come on, Joe. Let's go. You're ready, ¹_____

Boy   Yes, Mum. It's only 8 o'clock, ²_____

Mum   No, it's ten past. You've got your schoolbag,
      ³_____

Boy   Yes, Mum.

Mum   And don't forget your football kit, ⁴_____

Boy   No, Mum.

Mum   You'll come straight home after school, ⁵_____

Boy   No, I'm going to Mandy's. I told you, ⁶_____

Mum   No, you didn't, but that's OK.

4 Write tag questions.

1 A I'm not keen on grapes.

   B ___Aren't you?___ Would you like an apple then?

2 A The boss wants to speak to you immediately.

   B _____ I wonder what she wants.

3 A I must leave soon.

   B _____ I'll get your coat then.

4 A Ben won't do his homework.

   B _____ I'll have a word with him.

5 A Everyone has gone home.

   B _____ They forgot to turn out the lights.

6 A I might buy a new car next week.

   B _____ Have you sold your old one?

7 A It's started to snow.

   B _____ We'd better wrap up warm.

8 A Nobody replied to my letter of complaint.

   B _____ That's shocking.

9 A Mark crashed his car yesterday.

   B _____ Is he OK?

10 A Liam is planning to row across the Atlantic.

   B _____ He must be mad.

11 A Fiona hadn't locked the car.

   B _____ No wonder it was stolen.

12 A Everything is fine.

   B _____ I'll leave you to it, then.

Extra Practice

Expressing opinions

I can express my opinions about a variety of subjects.

1 Complete the phrases for emphasising a point. Use the words in the box.

> bear believe convinced deny doubt forget
> remember think

1 We must _____ that …
2 There's no _____ in my mind that …
3 Let's not _____ that …
4 I _____ very strongly that …
5 It's important to _____ in mind that …
6 I'm absolutely _____ that …
7 Nobody can _____ that …
8 I really do _____ that …

2 Which of these sentences are opinions and which are examples that support opinions? Write O or E.

1 Babies and toddlers should be looked after at home not sent to nurseries. ☐
2 The air in city centres where cars are banned is much cleaner. ☐
3 Some countries have benefited greatly from membership of the EU. ☐
4 The UK government doesn't spend enough money researching alternative energy sources. ☐
5 It's been shown that children who are cared for at home when they are very young do better at school. ☐
6 People should use public transport rather than their cars. ☐
7 Only 5% of electricity in the UK is generated from renewable sources. ☐
8 The country has received a lot of money to build new roads. ☐

3 Match each opinion in exercise 2 with an example.

Opinion ☐1☐   Example ☐
Opinion ☐   Example ☐
Opinion ☐   Example ☐
Opinion ☐   Example ☐

4 🎧11 Listen to two students. Which of these four questions are they answering? Is their opinion 'yes', 'no' or 'undecided'?

1 Should we encourage more girls to do science at school? Why? / Why not?
2 Should the law prevent people under the age of 21 from buying cigarettes? Why? / Why not?
3 Has membership of the European Union been good for Poland? Why? / Why not?
4 Should we ban cars from all city centres? Why? / Why not?

Student A
Question _____   Yes ☐ No ☐ Undecided ☐

Student B
Question _____   Yes ☐ No ☐ Undecided ☐

5 Look at the sentences from the listening below. Find words or phrases that:

a introduce a personal opinion _____
b concede an argument _____
c mean 'without doubt' _____
d mean 'generally speaking' _____

A Personally, I really enjoy physics but it seems, on the whole, that boys enjoy science subjects more than girls.
B Admittedly, cars cause a lot of pollution and the air would undoubtedly be much cleaner if we didn't drive so much.

6 Prepare to give your opinion on question 2 or 3 in exercise 4. Write notes. Use one or more of the phrases in exercise 1 to emphasise the points you make, and think of an example to back up your opinion.

_____
_____
_____
_____
_____

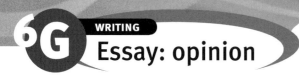

6G WRITING
Essay: opinion

I can write an opinion-based essay.

Preparation

1 Read the exam task and the essay. Why isn't it a very good model?

1 The introduction is too short. ☐
2 The writer's opinion isn't clear. ☐
3 The essay is too short. ☐
4 There are a lot of grammar and spelling mistakes. ☐
5 The writer only states his/her opinion and doesn't give arguments supporting the opposite opinion. ☐
6 The style is too informal. ☐
7 The conclusion is too short. ☐

Write an essay of 200–250 words on the following topic:
We have become too reliant on computers. Do you agree?

Nowadays almost every aspect of our lives is affected by computers. Some people think that computers can solve almost any problem, but I believe that we rely too much on them.

Firstly, if a computer that controls vital equipment in a large organisation breaks down, the consequences can be very serious. For example, if the computers in hospitals or air traffic control crash, then many lives could be lost.

Secondly, in the modern world, too many decisions are taken by computers and not by people. We will eventually lose our ability to make judgements for ourselves. What is more, computers are replacing people and taking their jobs. For example, online shops will eventually replace real shops and lots of people will lose their jobs.

Thirdly, computers are changing the way we live. Children rely too much on computers for entertainment. They spend hours playing games on the computer and forget how to play with other children or amuse themselves. They don't learn how to be creative – they just have to click the mouse and press keys.

To sum up, I believe that we have become too reliant on computers.

197 words

---

2 Write C next to the phrases for contrasting points, and A next to those for making additional points.

And yet, ... ☐ Furthermore, ... ☐ Having said that, ... ☐
However, ... ☐ Moreover, ... ☐ Nevertheless, ... ☐
On the other hand, ... ☐ Similarly, ... ☐
We should also remember that ... ☐ What is more, ... ☐

3 Complete the expressions with the words in the box.

balance	clear	deny	having	maintain	though
worth					

1 It is also hard to _____ that ...
2 _____ said that, it is true that ...
3 It is _____ that ...
4 It is also _____ bearing in mind that ...
5 Even _____ in some cases ... I would still _____ that in most cases ...
6 However, on _____, I believe that ...

4 Read the essay title. What is your initial reaction? Do you: ✔ agree with the statement? ✘ disagree with the statement?

Computers have made the world a better and safer place. Do you agree? ☐

5 Think of two or three points that support your opinion. Make notes in your notebook.

6 Think of one or two points that support the opposite opinion. Make notes.

7 Write your essay (200–250 words), following the plan in the writing guide below.

Writing Guide

Paragraph 1
Introduction. Explain the title and give your initial opinion.

Paragraph 2
First argument in support of your opinion.

Paragraph 3
Second argument in support of your opinion.

Paragraph 4
Arguments supporting the opposite opinion.

Paragraph 5
Summary including a re-statement of your opinion.

CHECKLIST

Have you:
- followed the writing plan?
- written 200–250 words?
- included examples that support your arguments?
- checked the spelling and grammar?

Extra Practice

EXAM TASK – Reading

Read the following article about online survey websites. Some parts of the text have been removed. Complete the text by matching the sentences (A–G) to the gaps in the text (1–6). There is one letter which you do not need to use.

You must have seen those online survey websites. They are slick and inexpensive. They have neat interfaces that let you create your own survey and invite others to participate; they can make you look really talented and impress others. ¹____ It certainly sounds like the results of these surveys provide real information that can be used in the decision-making process.

²____ There's no guarantee that the survey you create is reliable. And if it can't be proven reliable, you can't prove that its results are valid.

Without being reliable and valid, any survey is worthless. In simple terms, reliability means the results would look the same if you repeated the survey with the same people the next day. Validity means your instrument measures what you say it measures and not something else. ³____ At least with the latter, you know when it stops working. A questionnaire, on the other hand, will always produce numerical results, even if they're meaningless. ⁴____

For as long as questionnaires and surveys have existed, it has been known that you can't just throw a bunch of statements together with some agree/disagree scales, and come up with accurate comprehensive data. ⁵____ And many behavioural scientists, who ought to know better, have become willing accomplices by sponsoring these sites and promoting their use.

The same IT industry did amazing things with the automobile engine, with internal computers that monitor engine functioning and optimize timing and ignition while we drive. ⁶____ But the same sophistication has not been built into the typical online questionnaire. Just because the survey provider doesn't talk about it does not mean it is all being taken care of somewhere inside the computer.

So if you are considering a serious project and need to base it on reliable survey data, remember that a quick, 'cost effective' online survey may actually cost you much more.

A However, the Internet has allowed some IT people to turn the process of designing and implementing surveys into a 'do-it-yourself' activity.

B We do have to be aware of the difference between a 'do-it-yourself' survey and one with reliability and validity.

C Some have catchy tag lines like 'The easiest way to ask, the fastest way to know', or 'Because knowledge is everything'.

D We're now able to drive 100,000 miles without thinking about when we need to 'tune' the engine.

E But there's that 'dirty little secret' they don't want you to know about the surveys and questionnaires produced by non-specialists.

F An unreliable questionnaire is worse than an unreliable car.

G As a result, you could be making serious decisions based on survey results that don't mean anything.

EXAM TASK – Use of English

Complete the text with the correct words (A–D).

A noisy parrot called Peanut, who likes to imitate sounds, helped save Kenny Donovan and his four-year-old son from a house fire by mocking the ¹____ of a smoke alarm. The two had ²____ asleep on the sofa in the living room of their semi-detached house in Birmingham ³____ watching a movie. After hearing Peanut ⁴____ the fire alarm they awoke to find their home on fire. 'He was really screaming his head off,' Kenny said. The smoke alarm had gone ⁵____, but it was the bird's call that caught Kenny's attention. Grabbing his son and his bird, he safely got them out of the house. The fire, ⁶____ destroyed the kitchen and bedroom, ⁷____ under investigation. ⁸____ Peanut, it was the fact that they fell asleep downstairs on the sofa that helped save them. They may not ⁹____ the alarm or the bird if they ¹⁰____ asleep in their bedrooms, where an air conditioner drowns out most of the noise around the house.

	A	B	C	D
1	sound	noise	shout	call
2	fall	felt	fallen	feel
3	during	from	while	as
4	imitating	to imitate	imitated	has imitated
5	on	out	up	off
6	what	which	however	that
7	stays	remains	stands	returns
8	Beside	Aside from	Out of	Next to
9	heard	hear	had heard	have heard
10	were	would be	had been	have been

🎧 12 You will hear part of an interview with a famous literary critic. Read statements 1–7. Then listen and decide if each statement is true (T) or false (F) according to the information you hear.

		True	False
1	The author of *A Short History of Nearly Everything* did not like science when he was a student.		
2	Bill Bryson is a popular guidebook writer.		
3	In order to write the book, Bryson interviewed many scientists.		
4	The book they discuss concentrates on historical events.		
5	The book contains anecdotes about various scientists.		
6	Marcus believes the only problem with the book is that the language is too scientific.		
7	The interviewer has already read the book.		

PREPARATION: Writing
Use the Writing Bank on page 107 to help you.

A British travel agency has published an advertisement in *Travel Times* and is looking for people to work as restaurant and bar staff on their cruise ships in Scandinavia. Write a letter of application of 210–230 words to the manager of the travel agency.

In your letter include:
- personal information
- why you would like to work for them
- useful personal qualities
- relevant work experience

Write your letter in the appropriate style and format.

PREPARATION: Speaking
Use the Functions Bank on page 102 to help you.

Part 1 – Short interview

Work in pairs. One of you plays the role of the student, the other of the teacher/examiner. Start with Set 1, then exchange roles and continue with Set 2.

Role 1 – the student
Do not read the questions. Listen carefully to your partner and answer all his/her questions in detail. If you do not understand, ask your partner to repeat the question.

Role 2 – the teacher
Your role is to read each question to your partner. Choose 3–5 questions from the list below. Give your partner enough time to answer each of them.

Set 1 – Topic: Foreign languages
- Why do you study English?
- Is it important to study more than one foreign language? Why (not)?
- Which jobs require a good knowledge of foreign languages? Explain.
- What is an ideal language lesson for you?
- Would you like to improve your language knowledge? Why (not)?
- Would you like to study abroad? Where? What? Why (not)?

Now change roles and use the questions in Set 2.

Set 2 – Topic: The Internet
- Why do people of your age use the Internet?
- Do you think that the Internet plays an important role in today's society? Why (not)?
- What are the alternatives to the Internet (other sources of information)? Are they useful today? Why (not)?
- Can you imagine life without the Internet? Explain.
- What are the possible dangers/disadvantages of the Internet?
- What do you think about online dating?

7 Putting the world to rights

A **VOCABULARY**
Global warming

I can talk about the reasons for and consequences of global warming.

1 Complete the facts with the words in the box.

> atmosphere   caps   carbon CO_2 Earth
> emissions   energy   footprint   industrialised
> sea   solar   warming

Climate Facts

FACT! Each year, humans add about 30 billion tonnes of [1]_____ into the [2]_____ but half of it is absorbed by the forests and oceans.

FACT! Scientists are working on a way to collect [3]_____ power from space and send it back to [4]_____ as a giant laser beam.

FACT! Global [5]_____ is causing the ice [6]_____ to melt and the [7]_____ levels to rise – and they're rising faster because water expands as it gets warmer.

FACT! [8]_____ countries are currently only responsible for about 50% of carbon [9]_____, but they are responsible for 80% of the man-made CO_2 that is already in the atmosphere.

FACT! Leaving your DVD player on standby produces the same [10]_____ emissions each year as the average citizen of Burundi.

FACT! Being a vegetarian reduces your carbon [11]_____ (the amount of emissions caused by one person's lifestyle) because the production of meat and dairy products uses a lot of [12]_____.

2 Choose the correct word to complete the collocations in these sentences. Then read the sentences and circle T (true) or F (false).

1 Wind power is a type of fossil **fuel / power**.　　T　F
2 The majority of the Earth's fresh water is contained in the ice **caps / levels**.　　T　F
3 Trees and plants help to increase the greenhouse **warming / gases** in the atmosphere.　T　F
4 Petrol is a form of **recyclable / renewable** energy.　　T　F
5 The destruction of forests has led to an increase in the number of **dangerous / endangered** species.　T　F
6 Climate **change / warming** will create more extreme weather conditions.　T　F
7 Solar **waves / panels** generate electricity.　　T　F

3 Explain how each of these things is good or bad for our planet. Include the word in bold.

1 energy-saving light bulbs　**electricity**
They are good because they use less electricity than normal light bulbs.

2 wind turbines　**clean**
They are _____ because _____

3 tumble dryers　**electricity**
They are _____ because _____

4 long-haul flights　**carbon emissions**
They are _____ because _____

5 recyclable packaging　**household waste**
It is _____ because _____

● ● ● ● ● ● **CHALLENGE!** ● ● ● ● ● ●
Suggest three changes that could be made to your school to reduce its carbon footprint.

1 _____
_____
2 _____
_____
3 _____
_____

1 Decide what the underlined part of each sentence means and circle a or b.

1 <u>You really must try</u> these biscuits – I made them.
   a It's absolutely necessary that you try …
   b I really think you should try …

2 <u>You don't have to eat your sandwiches</u> in the canteen at our school.
   a It isn't necessary to eat your sandwiches …
   b It's against the rules to eat your sandwiches …

3 <u>You mustn't wear boots</u> in the house.
   a It isn't necessary to wear boots …
   b It's against the rules to wear boots …

4 <u>We ought to spend less</u> on phone calls.
   a It's very important to spend less …
   b It would be a good idea to spend less …

5 <u>They have to move house</u> before the end of the year.
   a It's obligatory for them to move house …
   b It's a good idea for them to move house …

2 Complete the advice with a suitable modal verb.

1 'You _____ tell Holly about passing your driving test. She might ask for lifts all the time.'

2 'You really _____ remember to switch the lights off at night, otherwise you waste electricity.'

3 'I don't think you _____ walk home alone – it's too dangerous.'

4 'If you're in Barcelona, you simply _____ see the Gaudi buildings.'

5 'No wonder you're sleepy. You _____ stay up so late!'

3 Give an example of something that you …

1 have to do but hate doing.

_____

2 don't have to do, but enjoy doing.

_____

3 ought to do often, but only do occasionally.

_____

4 should do less.

_____

5 mustn't do at home.

_____

4 Complete the dialogue with the words in the box. Use each word once.

don't have	have to	must	mustn't	need
needn't	should	shouldn't		

Going Places

Jake   Let's pick up some holiday brochures.
Cathy   Holiday brochures? Why?
Jake   We [1]_____ to book our summer holiday soon or all the good deals will have been taken.
Cathy   OK, but we [2]_____ to get brochures – they're a waste of paper. We [3]_____ search online. It's better for the environment.
Jake   If you're so worried about the environment, we [4]_____ go on holiday at all. Flying produces lots of CO_2!
Cathy   Who said anything about flying? We [5]_____ fly anywhere. I'm thinking of a walking holiday in Belgium. I've already found a company online that organises tours.
Jake   Look, you [6]_____ book anything without discussing with me first. Do you understand?
Cathy   Actually … it's already booked. Sorry!
Jake   Well phone up and cancel it! Even if you [7]_____ pay a fine, cancel it!
Cathy   Calm down! I was joking. You really [8]_____ try to develop a sense of humour.

5 Complete these sentences with your own ideas. Use a suitable modal verbs.

1 If you want to learn Mandarin, you _____
   _____ .

2 No wonder you can't sleep. You _____
   _____ .

3 Don't just sit there looking miserable. You _____
   _____ .

4 If the girl / boy of your dreams won't pay you any attention, you _____
   _____ .

5 If you want to lead a long and healthy life, you _____
   _____ .

Extra Practice

7C

CULTURE

Our vanishing planet

I can understand an article about environmental issues.

Revision: Student's Book page 73

1 Complete the sentences with the words in the box.

> coral   outcry   global   growth   interest
> primeval   species   vehicles

1 Conservationists are working to protect endangered _____ around the world.
2 Much of the jungle in the Congo is _____ forest.
3 A rise in sea temperatures will damage the world's _____ reefs.
4 Carbon emissions tend to increase in line with economic _____ .
5 Nearly all scientists today accept that _____ warming is a reality.
6 The revelation that toxic waste is being exported to developing countries has caused a public _____ .
7 Many old buildings in the village have been damaged by the heavy goods _____ that pass through.
8 The 'green' movement includes various _____ groups such as Greenpeace and Friends of the Earth.

2 Read the text quickly, ignoring the gaps. According to the writer, what is the answer to the question in the title?

_____

3 Complete each gap in the text with a suitable word.

4 Are these sentences true or false? Write T or F.

1 Even people who care about the environment are reluctant to give up flying. ____
2 People would make fewer flights if the government encouraged them to fly less often. ____
3 The British are gradually reducing the number of short flights that they make. ____
4 Short-haul flights create a quarter of the UK's total carbon emissions. ____
5 Compared to a decade ago, fewer destinations are available today for low-cost flights from the UK. ____
6 The leader of the study had not expected to find so much hypocrisy. ____

What's green and flies?

City Breaks: Prague from £140
London to Krakow from £170
Barcelona from £80 retu

They insist [1]_____ buying organic food and recycling every last scrap of paper or glass – and they're not slow to tell you about it. But when it comes [2]_____ giving up their trips to Krakow and weekend breaks in Prague, it seems that even the 'greenest' people in the UK are reluctant to make the sacrifice.

A study by Exeter University has revealed the huge number of supposedly environmentally-friendly Britons who refuse to give up low-cost flying in spite [3]_____ the damage to the planet. The authors of the study say this 'eco-hypocrisy' shows [4]_____ difficult it will be for governments to reduce greenhouse gas emissions by urging people to cut down on air-travel.

Environmental campaigners argue that cheap short-haul flights, [5]_____ are becoming more and more popular among the British, have caused a massive increase in carbon emissions over the past few years. Although pollution from flights accounts for just seven per cent of the UK's total greenhouse gas output, the figure [6]_____ predicted to reach 25 per cent over the next few decades.

Taking cheap flights to other European cities for a short holiday has become almost an addiction for the British over the past decade or so. Among [7]_____ most popular destinations are Kraków, Budapest, Prague, Brussels and Barcelona, and the low-cost airlines are adding new cities to the list all the time. Tickets cost [8]_____ little as €80 for a return flight, so you don't have to be well-off to travel abroad several times a year.

Dr Stewart Barr, [9]_____ led the focus group study, said that, although the study was based on only 64 people, the findings reflected a widespread trend. 'Most [10]_____ the committed environmentalists said they still travelled on low-cost airlines, [11]_____ though they realised it was problematic,' he said. 'But they couldn't see a way around it. We were surprised because we thought that people would transfer their attitudes towards environmentalism in the home to their holidays, but the difference was more striking [12]_____ we had imagined. The UK's addiction to cheap flights looks hard to break.'

Unit 7 • Putting the world to rights   **59**

Waste not, want not

I can understand an article about food waste.

Revision: Student's Book page 74–75

1 Choose the correct preposition in these sentences.

1 Is the government to blame **of** / **for** the amount of traffic on our roads?

2 She wasn't impressed **by** / **of** my efforts to lead a greener lifestyle.

3 At university, I specialised **at** / **in** Environmental Studies.

4 The Soil Association is committed **in** / **to** promoting organic food in the UK.

5 I beckoned **for** / **to** the waiter, but he ignored me.

6 The government does not allow journalists to have access **in** / **to** their plans for nuclear power.

7 She found it hard to cope **for** / **with** three young children while her husband was out at work.

8 The UK's annual CO_2 emissions from aviation are about 37 million tonnes, which amounts **in** / **to** 7% of its total emissions.

9 We should deal **at** / **with** the problem of climate change before it gets out of hand.

2 What is a 'freegan'? Choose the best definition.

a Somebody who collects food that supermarkets throw away and gives it to people who need it.

b Somebody who grows their own food instead of buying it.

c Somebody who eats food that has been thrown away as a protest against consumerism.

d Somebody who refuses to pay for food as a protest against capitalism.

3 Look through the text, ignoring the gaps. What is the main objective of the SWAG campaign?

a To encourage people to cook in more imaginative ways.

b To encourage people to spend less money in supermarkets.

c To encourage people to put less of the food they buy in the bin.

d To encourage people to recycle more of their household rubbish.

4 Read the text carefully. Match sentences A–G with gaps 1–6. There is one sentence that you do not need.

A Within that, there is more of an awareness, especially from the people who lived through the Second World War.

B For this reason, consumers are reluctant to alter their shopping habits, in spite of the evidence.

C Freeze leftovers so that they can be eaten at a later date.

D These are members of the public who aim to share their practical hints and tips to help avoid food waste.

E It offers tips, hints and simple recipes which enable people to make the most of the food they buy and prepare.

F Most is dumped in landfill, where it gives off greenhouse gases.

G Think about the meals for the week and check cupboards before going shopping.

5 Match the two halves of these expressions from the text.

1	to launch	a	the environment
2	to have an impact on	b	20% of the total
3	to come up with	c	an idea
4	to make	d	a campaign
5	to make up	e	improvements

6 Do older members of your family have a different attitude to wasting food? Give an example, and say why you think the difference may exist.

_____
_____
_____
_____
_____

●●●●●● CHALLENGE! ●●●●●●

Think of a dish which uses left-over food (for example, cooked meat, cooked potato or other vegetables). Write a short recipe or description.

_____
_____
_____
_____
_____
_____
_____
_____
_____

War on waste

People in the UK throw away about a third of the food they buy. Food waste makes up nearly 20 per cent of the total household bin – and around half of this could actually have been eaten. Not only does this cost consumers a huge amount of money, but it also damages the environment. Firstly, there is the damage caused by producing the unnecessary food in the first place. And secondly, there is the fact that all the food we throw away creates hundreds of tones of domestic waste. [1]_____ Experts say preventing the waste would have the same impact as removing one in five cars from the road.

Now, various organisations are trying to crack down on food waste. For example, a campaign has been launched north of the border by SWAG (the Scottish Waste Awareness Group), with the support of leading chefs and food writers. They are focusing on four key areas where improvements can be made: planning meals, storing food properly, using up leftovers and buying accurate amounts.

Dr Nicki Souter, SWAG's campaign director, said: 'Attitudes to food waste are very similar across the age groups, apart from the 60-plus generation. [2]_____ But if you look at the adult population as a whole, typically we waste a lot of food. Every time we cook rice or pasta, it's difficult to get the portion size right.

The aim of this campaign is to get the public thinking about the issue of food waste and ultimately doing something to limit the problem.'

Another organisation which is campaigning on the same issue is called Love Food Hate Waste. According to the campaign, the key foods wasted in the home are fresh fruit and vegetables, meat and fish, bakery and bread products and dairy products. The main reasons are preparing too much food or letting it go past its use-by date. And the campaign says 90 per cent of people do not even realise how much is being disposed of.

The Love Food Hate Waste campaign has come up with the idea of having 'champions'. [3]_____ There is also a website to raise public awareness. [4]_____ Here is a selection of the practical advice on offer:

- Portion sizes: Buy loose fruit and vegetables to get the exact amount that you need. Look out for smaller size options and measure portion sizes when you cook.
- Planning: [5]_____ . That way you won't buy food that is already in your fridge!
- Storage: Learn the difference between use-by dates, where the food can go off quickly, and best-before dates, which tend to affect quality rather than safety. Follow the storage instructions on food, and rotate the food in the fridge and cupboard so that you know what needs using first. [6]_____
- Recipe ideas: Use leftovers and check the campaign website for tips. For example, leftover vegetables and potato can be fried together with bacon and onion to make a traditional British dish called 'bubble and squeak'!

Bubble and squeak

7E GRAMMAR
Speculating: present, past and future

I can speculate about events.

1 Underline the modal verb in each sentence and decide whether it refers to the past, present or future.

1 We'd better take an umbrella. It <u>might</u> rain. <u>future</u>

2 Where does Connor live? Grace may know – I'll ask her. _____

3 She can't have a brother – she told me she was an only child. _____

4 Ask at reception. They might have found your passport. _____

5 By the time we reach the airport, it could be too late! _____

2 Complete the sentences with *must, might* or *can't*.

1 She _____ go to this school. I've never seen her before.

2 Look, it's already dark outside. It _____ be later than we realised.

3 This _____ be my phone, it's red. Mine has a green case.

4 £3.75 for a coffee? You _____ be serious!

5 You _____ be exhausted. You've been working for nearly six hours without a break.

6 I'm not sure whose laptop this is. It _____ belong to my aunt.

7 Dan and Ali haven't arrived yet. They _____ be lost.

8 Aunt May called. She _____ come by tomorrow if she has time.

3 Continue each sentence in your own words.

1 Bella's crying. Somebody must have _____

_____

2 You got less than 10% in your exam. You can't have _____

_____

3 I'm not sure where Tilly is. She may have _____

_____

4 Judy hasn't phoned me for weeks. She must have _____

_____

5 The restaurant has gone out of business. They can't have

_____

6 Witnesses saw strange lights in the sky. They might have

_____

4 Complete the dialogue with *must (have)*, *might / may / could (have)*, and *can't (have)* and the verbs in the box.

be	be	break into	go	leave	look	need	open

Jake   That's strange. My mum isn't here, but the window's open.

Cathy   She [1]_____ it for some fresh air and then gone out, I suppose.

Jake   She's usually really careful about things like that. She [2]_____ the house in a real hurry.

Cathy   I hope everything's OK. Look at those muddy footprints on the floor!

Jake   I'll phone my mum. Hmm. Her phone's switched off.

Cathy   Have you any idea where she [3]_____?

Jake   She's often out at this time. She [4]_____ to work – or to the gym.

Cathy   I think she [5]_____ to come home as soon as possible.

Jake   Why?

Cathy   Well, there's only one explanation for the open window and the footprints. A burglar [6]_____ your house!

Jake   You're right. Actually, look at these footprints. They [7]_____ mine or my mum's, They're too big.

Cathy   If I were you, I'd call the police. And don't touch anything! The police [8]_____ for the burglar's fingerprints.

●●●●●● CHALLENGE! ●●●●●●

Write three sentences about this photo. Use *might (have)*, *must (have)* and *can't (have)*.

1 _____

2 _____

3 _____

 Extra Practice

1 Label the pictures with the words in the box.

> bin   bins   burning   compost   cycle   panel   rack
> recycling   solar   stove   turbine   wind   wood

1

2

3

4

5

6

2 🎧 13 Listen to two students discussing ways to make their school greener. Which three items from exercise 1 do they describe?

1 _____
2 _____
3 _____

3 🎧 13 Listen again. Complete these extracts with the correct word.

1 What about those things that you put on the _____?
2 You know, for _____ electricity.
3 Wood is a renewable _____.
4 What about those metal _____ for burning wood in?
5 That way, we'd send less waste to _____ sites.

4 Choose the correct word in these sentences.

1 All new public buildings must use low *energy/power* light fittings.
2 My grandparents' home is much warmer since they installed double *glass/glazing*.
3 If you're thirsty, there's a *drink/drinking* fountain next to the steps.
4 Don't throw your empty bottles away! Put them in the recycling *bin/can*.

5 Put the nine items from exercises 1 and 4 into the correct group.

1 They are sources of energy.
_____
_____
_____

2 They help reduce energy consumption.
_____
_____
_____

3 They are an alternative to throwing rubbish away.
_____
_____
_____

4 They encourage 'greener' behaviour.
_____
_____
_____

6 Try to think of one more item for each group in exercise 5.

Essay: for and against

I can write a for and against essay.

Preparation

1 Read the task. Decide whether you agree or disagree with the statement.

'Making personal lifestyle changes will never stop global warming.' Do you agree or disagree?

2 Read the eight jumbled parts of the essay (a–h). Match them with the paragraph plan in column 2.

a Moreover, most 'green' choices have negative consequences as well as positive ones. For example, energy-saving light bulbs contain mercury, a poisonous metal that could pollute the environment when the bulbs are thrown away.

b However, others maintain that carbon emissions are increasing so quickly in developing countries, like China and India, that there is nothing we can do to prevent climate change.

c On the other hand, environmental campaigners argue that individual choices can make a big difference if millions of people act together. If everybody in the UK switched off their TV at night, it would reduce the amount of CO_2 released into the atmosphere by a significant amount.

d And while it's true that governments can do more than individuals, I feel that individuals definitely have an important role to play.

e Some people believe that we can reduce global warming if we all do our best to live a 'greener' lifestyle.

f Another argument in favour of changing your lifestyle is that we can't expect developing countries to care about their emissions unless the West sets a good example.

g It is argued that personal lifestyle choices can only make a tiny difference to a country's carbon emissions. For instance, using energy-saving light bulbs in your home makes an insignificant difference compared to the electricity that used by, say, a factory.

h On balance, I believe that individuals should do everything they can to reduce carbon emissions.

Paragraph plan

Paragraph 1 (Introduction) – a brief introduction to both sides of the argument:
1 ___*e*___ 2 _____

Paragraph 2 – arguments supporting the opposite view from your own:
3 _____ 4 _____

Paragraph 3 – arguments supporting your own view:
5 ___*c*___ 6 _____

Paragraph 4 (conclusion) – a summary of the issue and clear statement of your own view:
7 _____ 8 _____

3 Match the highlighted phrases in the essay with their equivalent phrases below.

1 In contrast ... _____
2 Furthermore ... _____
3 All in all ... _____
4 My view is that ... _____
5 Some people claim that ... _____
6 For example ... _____

4 Read the task. Decide whether you agree or disagree. Then make notes following the same paragraph plan as the one in exercise 2.

'To help prevent climate change, governments should ban individuals from flying more than once a year.' Do you agree or disagree?

5 Use your notes from exercise 4 to write an essay. Use the writing guide below to help you.

Writing Guide

1 Use phrases from exercise 3 to help structure each paragraph.
2 You don't have to summarise both sides of the argument in the introduction; you can give some background information about the topic instead.
3 Make sure the conclusion clearly states your own opinion, even if it mentions the opposite view.

CHECKLIST

Have you:
- followed the paragraph plan?
- included examples to support some of the points?
- checked your work for mistakes?

 Extra Practice

8 Caught in the net

A VOCABULARY
The Internet

I can describe how to use the Internet.

1 Find 15 more words associated with the Internet and computers in the wordsearch. (→↓)

W	C	O	M	M	A	N	D	R	T	Y	W
D	U	P	A	S	S	W	O	R	D	P	I
E	A	E	S	D	F	W	I	C	O	N	R
S	C	R	O	L	L	E	G	H	J	K	E
K	L	A	Z	X	C	B	V	B	B	N	L
T	M	T	H	U	M	B	N	A	I	L	E
O	Q	I	W	E	R	R	T	C	U	A	S
P	I	N	O	P	A	O	S	K	D	D	S
F	G	G	H	J	K	W	L	B	Z	D	N
X	D	S	A	V	E	S	C	U	D	R	E
V	R	Y	B	N	M	E	Q	T	O	E	T
P	J	S	S	W	M	R	F	T	C	S	W
W	G	T	R	T	Y	P	V	O	U	S	O
A	S	E	D	F	G	H	J	N	M	B	R
K	L	M	I	N	I	M	I	S	E	A	K
V	I	R	U	S	Z	X	C	V	N	R	B
N	M	Q	R	E	S	T	A	R	T	H	M

2 Match 1–12 with a–l and complete the sentences with words from the boxes.

> **address bar**   **minimise**   **operating system**   **scroll**
> **thumbnail**   **wireless network**

1 If the end of the document is hidden from view, ☐
2 To see a larger version of the photo, ☐
3 I used to use Windows XP, ☐
4 Are there wires running between your computer and modem, ☐
5 If you'd like to practise the vocabulary and grammar from this unit online, ☐
6 If you don't need to look at this webpage, ☐

a or are you connected to a _____ ?
b you need to _____ down.
c but you don't want to close it either, you can just _____ it.
d click on the _____ .
e type www.oup.com/elt/global/products/solutions/?cc=pl into the _____ .
f but now I use a different _____ .

> **desktop**   **drag**   **icon**   **password**   **restart**   **web browser**

7 After downloading a software update, ☐
8 When you buy a computer, ☐
9 I can't log on to the network because ☐
10 It's easier to keep track of documents ☐
11 To open the application, ☐
12 To attach the photo to the e-mail, ☐

g you usually get a free _____ such as Safari, Netscape or Internet Explorer.
h if you store them in folders on the _____ or in the hard drive.
i you'll probably need to _____ your computer.
j simply click on it and _____ it onto the window.
k click on the _____ on the desktop.
l I've forgotten my _____ .

●●●●● **Extension:** Phrasal verbs with *off* and *on*

3 Rewrite the sentences using the phrasal verbs in brackets.

1 Keep walking until you reach the traffic lights. (carry on)
_____

2 The strike was cancelled at the last minute. (call off)
_____

3 Take a chocolate and then give them to Ed. (pass on)
_____

4 Jodie left at five p.m. and arrived home at six. (set off)
_____

5 George agreed to do a lot of extra work because he needed the money. (take on)
_____

6 Don't disturb Jamie while he's concentrating. (put off)
_____

●●●●●● **CHALLENGE!** ●●●●●●

Describe in detail something you did on a computer and how you did it (e.g. downloading something, sending an attachment with an e-mail, etc.)
_____
_____
_____
_____

GRAMMAR
Modals in the past

I can use modal verbs to talk about the past.

1 Complete the text in the cartoons. Use a verb from the box and each of these modals verbs once: *might have, needn't have, ought to have* and *shouldn't have.*

book	bring	stay up	leave

① We're lost!

We _____ a map with us.

Kevin _____ all night playing computer games.

③ You _____ one for me.

④ You _____ our summer holiday last week.

2 Complete the sentences with a modal in the past and the verbs in brackets. Sometimes more than one answer is possible.

1 We got lost on the way. We turned left when we _____ _____ right. (turn)

2 I spent all morning looking for my camera. You _____ _____ me that you'd borrowed it! (tell)

3 Thanks for the sandwich, but you _____ _____ it. I had lunch in town. (make)

4 It only took fifteen minutes to get home because I _____ _____ long for a bus. (wait)

5 Josh _____ me know that he wasn't coming home. I cooked dinner for him. (let)

6 'I've got stomach ache.' 'Well, you _____ _____ all those chips.' (eat)

7 You _____ any milk. There's lots in the fridge. (buy)

8 Jeff lent me some money, so I _____ _____ any from the cash machine. (get)

3 Read the situations. What might the people have said? Write sentences using the words in brackets.

1 Jim didn't do very well in his school-leaving exams. (ought / do revision)
Jim's dad: <u>You ought</u> _____

2 Melanie bought Fred some new socks. Fred had already bought some the day before. (might / tell)
Melanie: _____

3 Jack went out without telling his parents. But he only went next door to see his friend. (needn't / worry)
Jack: _____

4 Harry thought he needed some petrol, but when he checked, the tank was full. (didn't need / fill)
Harry: _____

5 Jenny borrowed her sister's shoes without telling Anna. Anna was annoyed. (should / ask)
Anna: _____

Extra Practice

Social networking sites

I can understand and react to an article about social networking sites.

Revision: Student's Book page 83

1 Complete the text with words from the box. (You do not need to use all the words.)

> compulsion conclusion feature late launched
> networking personal options opt out plea
> protests users website

FaceBook is a social ¹_____ site popular with people in their ²_____ teens and early twenties. It allows ³_____ to upload information about themselves onto the ⁴_____, including photos and video. However, when a new ⁵_____ was ⁶_____ which automatically sent details of any changes to other users, FaceBook was inundated with ⁷_____ from members. Privacy ⁸_____ were quickly introduced allowing members to ⁹_____ of the new feature.

2 Complete the text with appropriate words.

3 Read the text. Are the sentences true or false?

1 Users of social networking sites could become victims of identity fraud. ____
2 Fraudsters are joining social networking sites and pretending to be someone else. ____
3 People often use the names of members of their family or of pets as passwords. ____
4 Approximately 10% of people in the UK think they have had their identities stolen. ____
5 Employers often use social networking sites to find information about people applying for jobs. ____
6 Information on social networking sites can only be read by other members of the website. ____

4 Find words in the text that mean:

1 a person who has been tricked _____
2 to get, especially by making an effort _____
3 things that can be bought _____
4 person who cheats somebody to get money _____
5 person who is applying for a job _____
6 to find new people to join a company _____

Be careful what you say

People ¹____ use social networking websites could ²____ putting themselves at risk of becoming victims ³____ identity theft. Identity fraud occurs when a criminal pretends ⁴____ be someone else and uses stolen personal details to obtain goods or services. One in five of the UK population now visit social networking sites, and more and ⁵____ consumers are signing up every day. The chances are that, when they register, they will enter their date ⁶____ birth, address, e-mail address, job, and marital status. Fraudsters can use this information ⁷____ steal an individual's identity and open a bank account or buy goods in their name. Giving away personal details ⁸____ as the names of your children or pets is particularly

risky since these are often used ⁹____ passwords. Identity theft is ¹⁰____ growing problem in the UK. About one ¹¹____ ten Britons claims to ¹²____ been the victim of identity theft, and it ¹³____ estimated that the crime costs the economy about £1.5 billion ¹⁴____ year.
Another potential problem is that social-networking sites have become a tool for potential employers. Twenty per cent ¹⁵____ UK companies routinely conduct web searches to find background information about the people ¹⁶____ are applying for jobs with them. They are sometimes able to check ¹⁷____ job applicants have described themselves honestly and accurately in their applications. Some employers also try to learn something about an applicant's personality and judge whether he or she is the kind ¹⁸____ person they would like to recruit.
Many of the young people who put photos and comments on these sites believe ¹⁹____ the information is private, or only read by the other members of the site. But if you use social networking sites and you are applying for a job, you'd do well to make sure there is nothing online that you would not like your prospective employer ²⁰____ see.

8D
READING
Another world

I can understand an article about online games.

Revision: Student's Book page 84–85

1 Complete the sentences with the words in the box.

advertisers   avatars   created   currency
imaginary   online games   software engineer
virtual worlds

1 Roo Reynolds' job is to play _____ .
2 Players of games like Second Life move and act in _____ which are populated by _____ .
3 Entropia Universe was _____ by a company called Mindark. It is based on the _____ planet of Calypso.
4 _____ are very interested in the virtual populations of online games.
5 Digital worlds often have their own _____ , such as the Linden Dollar.
6 The only full-time employee of Linden Lab is Jim Purbick, a _____ .

2 Read the text quickly. What is the problem with online games?

a People can become addicted to them.
b People spend all their money on them.
c Too many teenagers are playing them.

3 Read the text again and carefully choose the best answers.

1 A study has shown that …
A some of the players of online games gamble and take drugs.
B 11% of players are addicted to online games.
C people who play online games are depressed.
D 7,000 players showed signs of addiction.

2 According to the study …
A it is mostly children who experience addiction problems.
B gaming sites are too expensive for most people.
C the majority of gamers were adults.
D very few gamers are over 30.

3 The main problem with online games is …
A not enough women play them.
B too many people log on at the same time.
C it's impossible to switch off the computer while the game is in progress.
D people find it difficult to stop playing because the game never ends.

4 Online games are particularly dangerous for …
A people who may be predisposed to spending too much time playing.
B everyone who plays too much.
C people who don't have much money.
D people who don't understand the financial consequences of playing.

5 In some countries …
A compulsive gamers have to attend special clinics.
B compulsive gamers can be cured of their addiction.
C help is given to compulsive gamers.
D people are much less critical of online games.

6 Which sentence best sums up the conclusion of the study?
A Online games are essentially harmless.
B Everyone who plays too much will eventually become addicted.
C Online games should be banned.
D Online games are dangerous for a minority of people who play excessively.

7 Kevin from Liverpool …
A stopped playing online games because he had a problem with his computer.
B thinks that players can't tell the difference between virtual worlds and real world.
C thinks that you gain nothing from online games.
D thinks that fighting battles and killing dragons are great achievements.

8 Martin from Cardiff …
A thinks that playing online games is no worse than watching TV.
B thinks that people who watch a lot of TV also have a serious addiction.
C has been playing online games for five years.
D wishes he could play EverQuest again.

●●●●●● **CHALLENGE!** ●●●●●●
Do you play computer games online? Why? / Why not?

_____
_____
_____
_____
_____
_____

A DANGEROUS HABIT

The world of online gaming is a growing phenomenon with millions of young men and women around the globe logging on to join in role-play games which allow them to interact with other players. EverQuest and World of Warcraft are two of the biggest online games. Seven million people subscribe to World of Warcraft and join a virtual world of Lord of the Rings type characters.

However, a study of 7,000 online computer gamers has revealed that one in nine were displaying the same signs of addiction as gamblers and drug users. The subjects, mostly male and with an average age of 21, were asked to fill out two questionnaires. The addictive signs they displayed included withdrawal symptoms such as depression and craving, loss of control and neglect of other activities.

The results will prove alarming for parents whose children spend hours on the computer. EverQuest, a fantasy game in which players populate a virtual mystical world of dragons and wizards has proved to be particularly addictive, and has been blamed for marriage break-ups, child-neglect and even an obsessive player's suicide. An EverQuest widows'

support group has been set up for people who never see their partners because they are always playing the game.

The study is the work of Professor Mark Griffiths, director of the International Gaming Research Unit at Nottingham Trent University, in the UK. 'Addicted' gamers were compared to the remaining 'normal' players and it was found that they played for much longer periods and were 'significantly' more likely to report withdrawal symptoms. Last night Prof Griffiths said it was a largely adult phenomenon because most online gaming sites require a credit card subscription. (Fees are typically about £8 a month.) The average age of an online gamer is 29 to 30. However, he did find that some teenagers were playing, after parents subscribed to the sites. About 20 per cent of players are women, drawn by the social and co-operative element of the games.

'Although I think genuine addiction is fairly low, the thing about online gaming is that the game never stops,' said Prof Griffiths. 'With a stand-alone game, you can switch it off and come back the next day, but with an online game it's very difficult to log off when

you know half the world has just logged on. Many gamers play excessively and display few negative effects. There is nothing wrong in itself with doing something excessively, and unlike gambling, gaming has little or no financial consequence. However, the 24-hour a day never-ending online games may provide a potentially addictive medium for those with a predisposition for excessive game playing.'

In other parts of the world, such games have come in for much greater criticism. In China a girl died after playing World of Warcraft for three days with barely a break, and a woman in the USA blamed a game for the death of her 21-year-old son, who had a history of mental health problems, and shot himself while still sitting at his computer. In these countries a whole host of special treatments and clinics are available which claim to hold a cure for the compulsive gamer. In South Korea, the authorities have become so concerned by the numbers of young people spending too much time on computers that the government launched a nationwide addiction hotline to help combat the problem.

GAMING FORUM

Kevin, *Liverpool*
I used to play games every day, but last month I deleted every game on my computer and cancelled my subscription to Warcraft. The problem is that you get totally immersed in the games and become oblivious to the real world. What have you achieved after 11 hours in a virtual world? You might have developed your virtual character, fought a battle, killed a few dragons, but such achievements are illusory – when you return to the real world you're at exactly the same point as when you started.

Martin, *Cardiff*
I started playing EverQuest five years ago, and for the next two years the game dominated my life. But they were wonderful years and I have no regrets. I had the most amazing experiences and made loads of friends through the game. OK, so it's escapism, but how is it any different from watching TV? I know people who spend seven or eight hours a day watching TV but no one ever suggests they have a serious addiction.

Mixed conditionals

I can talk about the consequences of an imaginary event in the past or present.

1 Match the halves of these mixed conditional sentences.

1 If I hadn't lost my job, ☐

2 If I had a car, ☐

3 If I didn't live in Rome, ☐

4 If I hadn't asked you to dance at Joe's party, ☐

5 If I'd left earlier, ☐

a we wouldn't be going out now.

b we'd be able to afford a holiday.

c I'd be there now.

d it would have been more difficult to learn Italian.

e I'd have given you a lift to the station.

2 Complete these mixed conditional sentences with the correct form of the verbs in brackets.

Excusez moi, pouvez-vous me dire ...

1 If I _____ (pay) more attention in French classes when I was at school, I _____ (understand) what that man is saying.

2 She _____ (not be) at this school now if her parents _____ (not move) to this town three years ago.

3 If I _____ (not like) pasta, I _____ (not have) it for dinner last night.

4 If I _____ (be) taller, I _____ (join) the police force when I left school.

5 You _____ (have) a lot of money now if you _____ (invest) wisely.

6 If it _____ (not be) so cold this morning, I _____ (not wear) my fur coat.

7 If you _____ (pay) attention, you _____ (can) work out the answer.

3 Read the situations and write mixed conditional sentences.

EXAM

1 I failed my maths exam last month. That's why I'm taking it again.

_____

2 I haven't got much money. That's why I didn't buy a new car.

_____

3 Dave didn't write to Emily. That's why she's cross with him.

_____

4 Bill is learning German. That's why he spent the summer in Munich.

_____

5 Poland beat Belgium. That's why they're playing in the European Cup.

_____

6 Ellen hasn't got a mobile. That's why she couldn't phone you last night.

_____

7 Harry lost his iPod. That's why he's looking miserable.

_____

8 Madeleine isn't feeling well. That's why she didn't go to school yesterday.

_____

 Extra Practice

8F SPEAKING
Discussion

I can discuss my opinions of newspaper stories.

1 Complete the expressions using the words in the box.

completely	couldn't	disagree	how	of
opposite	really	right	see	spot	think	way

1 a I agree _____. ☐
   b I _____ agree more. ☐
2 a That's what I _____ too. ☐
   b That's how I _____ it too. ☐
3 a I think you're absolutely _____. ☐
   b I think you're _____ on. ☐
4 a I totally _____. ☐
   b I _____ can't agree with you. ☐
5 a I take the _____ view. ☐
   b I'm _____ the opposite opinion. ☐
6 a That's not _____ I see it at all. ☐
   b That's not the _____ I look at it. ☐

2 🎧 14 Listen. What are the people discussing in each conversation? Match the questions with the conversations and decide if the people agree or disagree with each other.

a Are computer games bad for you?
   Conversation _____ Agree / Disagree
b Should there be computers in every classroom?
   Conversation _____ Agree / Disagree
c Do young people spend too much time using computers?
   Conversation _____ Agree / Disagree
d Will computers soon be more intelligent than humans?
   Conversation _____ Agree / Disagree
e Was the world a better place before the invention of computers?
   Conversation _____ Agree / Disagree

3 🎧 14 Listen again. Tick the expressions in exercise 1 that you hear.

4 Read the story below. Do you agree or disagree with these statements? Use expressions from exercise 1.

1 It was Oliver's fault.

2 Mr Coster shouldn't have left his son in the car.

3 Oliver should have been sitting in the back seat.

4 It was just an unlucky accident. No one was to blame.

5 The police should have arrested Mr Coster.

A toddler crashed his father's car into a parked police van after figuring out how to release the handbrake and take the car out of gear, putting it in neutral.

Jeffrey Coster left his three-year-old son Oliver in the car for just a couple of minutes while he went into a shop to buy some milk.

He left his young son in the front with his seat belt on. He had parked the car securely in gear, with the handbrake on and the front wheels turned towards the kerb. However, Oliver managed to imitate what he had seen his father do to release the handbrake, put the gear into neutral and steer it as it rolled down the hill, eventually hitting a police van parked nearby. The front of Mr Coster's car was damaged, but luckily Oliver was unharmed and it didn't cause any damage to the police van. Police saw the funny side and didn't arrest Oliver or his father.

5 Do you agree or disagree with these opinions? Use expressions from exercise 1.

1 We should spend less money on space exploration and more on helping people in developing countries.

2 Teenagers watch too much TV.

3 Men and women should share the housework.

Extra Practice

I can write the biography of a person.

Preparation

1 Complete the sentences with the words in the box. (There are two extra words.)

company	designed	employed	entrepreneur
launched	graduated	grew up	website

The co-founder of YouTube

Chad Hurley was born in 1977 and ¹_____ in Pennsylvania. He ²_____ from high school and went on to study Fine Art at university. He was hired as a graphic designer by PayPal in 1999 and ³_____ their current logo. As he didn't wish to work for PayPal any longer, he left the ⁴_____ in 2002. He found it difficult to send video clips by email, so he designed a ⁵_____ for sharing videos. YouTube was ⁶_____ in 2005 and is now one of the most popular websites in the world.

2 Rewrite each sentence in exercise 1 using an adverbial participle clause.

1 *Born in* _____

_____

2 _____

_____

3 _____

_____

4 _____

_____

5 _____

_____

6 _____

_____

3 Turn the notes below about Steve Chen, another co-founder of YouTube, into a continuous text using time expressions from the box. (You may need to make other changes.)

At the age of 12, ...   By the time he was 15, ...
In [year] ...   Between [year] and [year] ...
That summer / autumn / spring / winter ...
Having completed ... ,   During this time, ...
After leaving school / university ...
When he left school / university ...
About a year / a month / six months later ...

Born: 1978, in Taiwan. Age 15: emigrated to the USA. 1993–6: attended high school. 1996: went to University of Illinois. Studied Computer Science. 1999: Worked for PayPal. Met Chad Hurley. May 2005: left PayPal, started to develop YouTube. December 2005: YouTube launched. Was immediate success. October 2006: Google bought YouTube for $1.6 billion. Age 27: was a millionaire.

Writing Guide

4 Research information about one of the people in the box. (They have all founded important websites or search engines.) Make notes under some of the headings below.

Jeff Bezos (Amazon)	Mark Zuckerberg (Facebook)
Pierre Omidyar (eBay)	Larry Page (Google)
Sergey Brin (Google)	Chris DeWolfe (MySpace)
Tom Anderson (MySpace)	David Filo (Yahoo)
Jerry Yang (Yahoo)	Jawed Karim (YouTube)

1 Introduction: *name, nationality? why have you chosen him/her?*

2 Birth and education: *born where/when? parents? school? university? good student?*

3 Early childhood experiences: *memorable events? historical background?*

4 Early experiences of work: *first job? other occupations?*

5 Main achievement: *give details and background.*

6 Other work: *give details and examples.*

7 Relationships, marriage and children.

5 Use your notes to write a biography (200–250 words) of the person.

CHECKLIST

Have you:
• written 200–250 words?
• divided your biography into paragraphs?
• included time expressions and adverbial participle clauses?
• checked the spelling and grammar?

Extra Practice

Get ready for your EXAM 4

• Reading • Use of English • Listening • Writing • Speaking

EXAM TASK – Reading

Read the article about emoticons. Then for questions 1–4 choose the best answer A, B, C or D, according to the text.

Twenty-five years after they were invented as a form of computer-geek shorthand, emoticons are now everywhere. The smiling, winking and frowning faces that inhabit the computer keyboard have evolved into a quasi-accepted form of punctuation. These sweet hieroglyphs have conquered both the young and the old, as our daily communication relies more and more on text rather than the spoken word. There was a time when emoticons seemed naively youthful. Yet nowadays, applied appropriately, emoticons can no longer be dismissed as juvenile. They come in handy in many adult social interactions, and help avoid serious miscommunications.

Psychologists say it is only natural. People instinctively look for signals of intimacy in the human face. This results from countless generations of evolution, during which people relied on these signs as life-or-death signals to survive. When infants are given a series of geometrical patterns, their eyes will naturally be drawn to those that seem to represent a face. Faced with the absence of facial expressions in e-communications we should make up for it by composing e-mails that make it clear through our language that we are being cheerful, but that of course happens only in the ideal world. And so we've turned to emoticons. At first glance it seemed that only the younger generation took to the little faces. But in fact, in a recent emoticon survey of 40,000 users of Yahoo Messenger, 52 per cent of the respondents were older than 30. Among those, 55 per cent said they use emoticons every day. 82 per cent considered women more likely to use emoticons. But for men, who have a hard time using terms of tenderness, emoticons can be very helpful in conveying the affection.

Emoticons have now entered even the most serious areas of life. One military veteran says that he uses plenty of emoticons in his communications even with admirals at the Pentagon, where they provide a certain cover for high-ranking leaders to comment on sensitive matters. 'A wink says quite a lot,' he says. 'It could be a thousand different things – but I know what it means. It's a kind of code.' Also on Wall Street, businessmen will use the term 'QQ' (from an emoticon symbolizing crying eyes) into conversation as a sarcastic way of saying 'boo hoo.'

Supposedly, it all started in 1982. Scott Fahlman, a professor of computer science, was linked to an electronic university bulletin board where computer enthusiasts posted their opinions. In one note a joke about elevators was misinterpreted by some as a safety warning. So Fahlman suggested using :-) as a way to indicate jokes

and :-(for serious remarks. Fahlman's 'joke markers' spread quickly and within a month or so techies at Xerox were circulating a list of strikingly sophisticated new emoticons. He never received a trademark for his invention, and never made a dime from it. Before long, emoticons had accomplished what Esperanto never could, a universal lingua franca.

1 In the past, emoticons were
   A perceived as rather childish.
   B used instead of punctuation.
   C causing some misunderstandings.
   D only smiling, winking and frowning.

2 The use of pictures representing the human face
   A helped people to survive in the past.
   B makes our e-mails more cheerful.
   C is spreading among the older generation.
   D is hard for men who are not affectionate.

3 Which of these sentences is true?
   A The Pentagon leaders refuse to comment on their use of emoticons.
   B In military communication emoticons can have special meanings.
   C Wall Street businessmen especially like the crying emoticon.
   D 'QQ' is a special Wall Street code emoticon.

4 Professor Fahlman
   A came up with the smiling emoticon because he liked jokes.
   B used his connections to spread the idea of emoticons.
   C first came up with the idea of using the smiling emoticon.
   D was a huge fan of the idea of a lingua franca and Esperanto.

EXAM TASK – Use of English

Complete the sentences with the correct form of the words in brackets.

1 The coral reef is _____ (THREAT) by changes in the climate caused by global warming.

2 The photographer was _____ (JUST) accused of harassing the star as all the accusations turned out to be false.

3 The _____ (MAJOR) of residents taking part in the survey agreed that airport noise was the greatest nuisance in this area.

4 In order to promote eco-friendly thinking, the school decided to participate in a _____ (COMPETE) to find the greenest primary school in the country.

5 Her _____ (COMPLAIN) about unfair treatment was disregarded as she did not support it with any proof.

Get ready for your Exam 4 73

🎧15 You will hear three volunteers talking about their work. Read questions 1–7 below. Then match the questions to the three speakers by marking ✗ in the correct box.

	Which person	Juliet (A)	Bill (B)	Evelyn (C)
1	has been involved in volunteering for the longest period of time?			
2	helps people from all age groups?			
3	has to rely on others in his/her work?			
4	doesn't need to contact the people he/she helps?			
5	combines his/her volunteer work with their job?			
6	helps people who are at home on their own?			
7	helps people who can't go out?			

PREPARATION: Writing
Use the Writing Bank on page 105 to help you.

EXAM TASK – Writing

There is a discussion in your school magazine about shopping facilities. You want to contribute by writing a short essay (210–230 words) discussing traditional and online shopping.

In your essay, discuss:
- shopping times
- shelf space/endless offers
- price comparisons
- other reasons for and against online shopping

Write your essay in the appropriate style and format.

PREPARATION: Speaking
Use the Functions Bank on page 102 to help you.

EXAM TASK – Speaking

Part 2 – Sustained long turn

Task 1: Look at these two pictures showing people commuting to work. Compare and contrast them.

These ideas may help you:
- Setting/location
- Emotions/feelings
- Advantages/disadvantages of each means of transport
- Environmental issues
- Other

Task 2: Read the quotation below and express your opinion on it.

These ideas may help you:
- Do you agree or disagree with the quotation? Why?
- Support your opinion with an example/your own experience.

> 'I travel not to go anywhere, but to go. I travel for travel's sake. The great affair is to move.'
> Robert Louis Stevenson

A VOCABULARY
Working life

I can talk about my working life.

1 Label the photos with words from the box.

brick-layer	civil servant	farmer	fast-food employee
miner	nurse	pilot	surgeon	

a

b

c

d

2 Look at the chart. Match jobs 1–4 with the other four jobs from exercise 1.

	1	2	3	4
It's usually well paid.			✓	✓
You often have to wear a uniform.		✓		✓
You deal with the general public.		✓		✓
You do a lot of paperwork.			✓	
You attend a lot of meetings.			✓	
You often work outdoors.	✓			
You work with your hands.	✓			✓

1 _____
2 _____
3 _____
4 _____

3 In your own words, explain the difference between these terms.

1 to hand in your notice / to get the sack

_____

_____

2 to resign / to retire

_____

_____

3 to do shift work / to work part time

_____

_____

4 to work full time / to work overtime

_____

_____

●●●●● **Extension:** The job market

4 Match the job adverts with the general fields below. Then name one other job in each field.

legal ☐   retail ☐   construction ☐   leisure ☐   health ☐

1 **Senior electrical engineer**
Must have proven track-record working on large and complex projects. Apply with CV. Salary in the region of £50K + benefits. _____

2 **Cosmetic surgery nurse**
Must be fully qualified and well organised, with relevant experience. Salary: £19,000 p.a. _____

3 **Senior solicitor**
Minimum 5 years' experience. Candidates should apply online in the first instance. Salary £38–50,000 depending on age and experience. _____

4 **Youth sports programme worker**
The successful candidate will be a self-starter, have good organisational skills and be capable of working in a team. Salary £28K per annum. _____

5 **Showroom assistant**
Must have good people skills as well as the ability to perform under pressure. Send CV and covering letter. Salary £20,000 plus bonus. _____

●●●●●●● **CHALLENGE!** ●●●●●●●

Write a job advertisement for the post of English teacher at your school. What general field does it belong to?

_____

_____

_____

Habitual behaviour (present and past)

1 Complete the text with *would* or *used to* and the verbs in the box. Use *used to* only when *would* is not correct.

get out	hate	leave	live	push	walk	work

Alex ¹_____ on the twelfth floor of a block of flats. Every morning, he ²_____ his flat around 8 o'clock in the morning and take the lift down to the ground floor. Then, he ³_____ to the bus stop and catches the bus to work. Because Alex ⁴_____ as a waiter in a busy restaurant, he was always tired when he finished work in the evening. But in spite of that, on arriving back at his block of flats and getting into the lift, Alex ⁵_____ the button to go only as far as the ninth floor. He ⁶_____ of the lift and walk slowly up the stairs to his flat on the twelfth floor. He ⁷_____ those stairs. So why did he do it?

2 Read the text in exercise 1. Can you explain Alex's behaviour? (Answer on page 120.)

_____

_____

3 Complete this description of what you normally do on Saturdays. Use *will* (or *won't*) for habitual behaviour.

On Saturdays, I'll usually get up at _____. Then _____

_____

_____. After that _____

_____. Later _____.

_____

4 Match the sentences that go together. Complete the second sentence with the present continuous for habits.

1 He's really ill-mannered. [c]
2 She's very unreliable. ☐
3 He's incredibly hot-headed. ☐
4 She's very naive. ☐
5 He's really big-headed. ☐
6 She's extremely tight-fisted. ☐

a (constantly / say) _____ how great he is.
b (always / make) _____ important decisions without thinking first.
c (always / be) *He's always being* rude to people.
d (continually / let) _____ other people pay for her, just to save money.
e (forever / miss) _____ appointments.
f (constantly / trust) _____ people who turn out not to be trust-worthy.

5 Write second sentences in a similar way to exercise 4. Use your own ideas.

1 He's very insecure. _____

_____

2 She's very argumentative. _____

_____

3 He's very grumpy. _____

_____

4 She's totally thoughtless. _____

_____

6 Match the sentences that go together. Complete them with *will* or *would*.

1 'I got the sack from my last job.' ☐
2 'My next-door neighbour thinks I fancy her.' ☐
3 'Jack's trainers smell awful.' ☐
4 'Lucy gave my guitar to a charity shop.' ☐
5 'My uncle's had another accident.' ☐

a 'Well you _____ keep calling round to see her.'
b 'Well you _____ play it until two in the morning.'
c 'Well he _____ ride his motorbike too fast.'
d 'Well you _____ turn up late every day.'
e 'Well he _____ wear them every day.'

⬤⬤⬤⬤⬤⬤⬤ **CHALLENGE!** ⬤⬤⬤⬤⬤⬤⬤

Complete these sentences in your own words.

1 I used to _____
but now _____

2 I didn't use to _____
but now _____

In search of a better life

I can understand an article and talk about migration.

Revision: Student's Book page 95

1 Choose the correct words to complete the sentences.

1 The USA accepts more **legal** / **lawful** immigrants than any other country in the world.

2 In the 18th century, immigrants were **dominantly** / **predominantly** from Ireland, Britain, Canada and Germany.

3 Many immigrants saw America as the 'land of **chance** / **opportunity**'.

4 There are many people of Polish **ancestral** / **ancestry** in the USA.

5 America became a '**melting** / **mixing** pot' of different races.

6 For millions, Ellis Island was the **doorway** / **gateway** to a new life.

7 Immigrants had to pass the inspection before setting foot on American **earth** / **soil**.

2 Read the text. Choose the best summary: a, b or c.

a Many Britons are moving to Australia because the quality of life there is better. However, it's difficult for them to find a good job.

b Australia is trying to attract British workers by convincing them that they will have a better life there. However, this could leave Britain short of several kinds of key workers.

c In the 1950s and 1960s, many Australians came to Britain to work. The situation is now reversed, and Britons are applying for work in Australia.

3 Are these sentences true or false? Write T or F.

1 There are not enough professionals in Australia to fill the available jobs. _____

2 Australia's sunny climate is being used to persuade British workers to emigrate. _____

3 Australia is only trying to attract office workers, not manual workers. _____

4 The normal immigration process will be made faster for people with the right qualifications. _____

5 The text suggests that many British workers will be keen to leave their family behind. _____

6 The text implies that if too many British workers emigrate, it will create problems in the UK. _____

IN SEARCH OF THE SUN

Australia wants to poach 20,000 British workers to solve a serious labour shortage. Professionals, from doctors and nurses to hairdressers and pastry chefs, are being invited to start a new life Down Under.

The publicity campaign shamelessly compares the British climate with Australia's 'glorious weather and miles of sandy beaches'. It is the most aggressive recruitment drive since a million Britons known as the 'Ten Pound Poms' — after the £10 fare they paid for the journey — emigrated to Australia in the fifties and sixties. ('Pom' is a colloquial Australian word for somebody from Britain.)

Among the workers Australia is seeking are electricians, carpenters, engineers, bricklayers, accountants and cabinet makers. Those who fit the criteria — in terms of age, skills and experience — will be fast-tracked for visas.

Oonagh Baerveldt, of the Australian Visa Bureau, said: 'It's often not a difficult decision to leave the British weather behind, but there are serious considerations with regard to leaving family and friends.'

There are also fears the latest scheme will deepen the crisis for the National Health Service and other British services already struggling under severe shortages of staff. Australia's plans could even create a hairdressing crisis, it was claimed. Ray Seymour, general secretary of the National Hairdressers' Federation, said: 'We have a shortage of skilled hairdressers and this is going to make it worse. But it's very sunny over there and there is a strong possibility that a lot of hairdressers will be tempted.'

•••••• CHALLENGE! ••••••

Imagine you were starting a campaign to attract skilled workers to your country. What would you say in order to encourage them to come?

_____

_____

_____

_____

9D READING
Making a name for yourself

I can understand an article about successful dropouts.

Revision: Student's Book page 96–97

1 Complete the summary of the text, *The Brit School* using the words in the box.

corridors	entertainment	fall	name
rehearse	scene	solo	state-funded

The Brit School is a ¹_____ secondary school where, in addition to all the normal subjects, the students also learn about the ²_____ industry and how to be successful in it. The ³_____ of the school are usually full of noise as the students ⁴_____ together. Most of them dream of being stars, but the school provides them with a good education to ⁵_____ back on in case their dreams do not come true. However, several former students of the Brit School are already making a ⁶_____ for themselves. These include Katy Melua, who recently completed a ⁷_____ tour of the USA, and the Kooks, who are an established part of the UK music ⁸_____ .

2 Look through the text quickly, ignoring the gaps. Did each person drop out of school or university?

1 Bill Gates dropped out of _____ .
2 Russell Simmons dropped out of _____ .
3 Uma Thurman dropped out of _____ .

3 Match sentences A–G with gaps 1–6. There is one sentence that you do not need.

A In fact, it is estimated that he has donated more than half his fortune to charities.
B She was unusually tall, with a sharp, angular face, big ears and very large feet.
C His father was a teacher and his mother was a recreation director.
D In fact, it was a lie: they hadn't written a single line of code.
E However, she returned to school later in order to take her exams.
F This is a special school which offers classes to children who are already pursuing a career in the performing arts.
G Just like that, I saw how I could turn my life in another, better way.

4 Complete these sentences about the three people in the text. Write Gates, Simmons or Thurman.

1 _____ dropped out of education because of a friend.
2 _____ could easily have ended up leading a life of crime.
3 _____ is involved in a lot of different kinds of businesses.
4 _____ boasted about some work before it had actually been done.
5 _____ received unkind comments from other children at school.
6 _____ started a fashion label and a record label.
7 _____ decided on a future career after one particular night.
8 _____ dropped out of two different schools.

5 Find words in the text that mean:

1 to obtain or achieve something, especially when this means using a lot of effort _____
2 working together with somebody in order to produce or achieve something _____
3 well known for being bad _____
4 a thing of value, especially property that a person or company owns _____
5 to be laughed at or made jokes about, either in a friendly way or maliciously for embarrassment _____
6 completing a course in education at high school or college _____

●●●●●● CHALLENGE! ●●●●●●
Find out about someone who has been successful 'against the odds'. Write a paragraph about them.

School Dropouts

For most people, a good education is the first step on the ladder of success. Whatever career you dream of pursuing, you are likely to need the right qualifications. Of course, there are always exceptions. Not every billionaire businessman or internationally famous celebrity began in a promising way!

Bill Gates

Bill Gates was a good student who managed to secure a place at Harvard University, often regarded as the best university in the world. However, he did not finish his degree. The main reason for this was that his childhood friend, Paul Allen, persuaded him to leave. At that time, PCs for the home had just been invented. One of the first models was called Altair, and was manufactured by a company called MITS. Paul Allen and Bill Gates wrote to MITS and told them that they had written a version of the programming language BASIC that was perfect for the Altair. ¹_____ When MITS asked for a demonstration, Gates and Allen worked fast, and wrote the software in just eight weeks. Soon, they were collaborating with MITS full time, and formed their own company, Microsoft. Today, Microsoft employs more than 64,000 people in 85 countries. Bill Gates is probably the richest person in the world and is widely considered to be the world's most generous humanitarian. ²_____

Russell Simmons

Russell Simmons was born into a respectable, middle-class family. ³_____ But Simmons rebelled. He abandoned school, joined a notorious gang, and started selling drugs on the street. But everything changed one night in 1977 when he saw a man called Eddie Cheeba performing a mixture of poetry and music to a wildly enthusiastic audience. (Of course, this kind of music later became known as rap and hip-hop.) In his autobiography, Simmons describes the moment like this: '⁴_____ I decided to put [everything] into promoting music.' Simmons became the 'godfather of hip-hop' and built a huge business empire around his record label, Def Jam. His fashion label, Phat Farm, is known around the world and he has also launched TV shows, a soft drink (DefCon3 soda), a new kind of Visa card and many other business projects. In total, his assets are valued at over $500 million.

Uma Thurman

Uma Thurman, glamorous star of Quentin Tarantino's *Kill Bill* films, was not always the epitome of female beauty. In fact, she was an odd-looking child. ⁵_____ At school other children teased her, and when she was ten years old, a friend's mother even suggested that she have cosmetic surgery to alter her nose. (Luckily, she ignored the advice.) By the age of 15, Thurman had decided that she found school boring, and she left to seek work as an actress. For a while, she continued her education at the Professional Children's High School. ⁶_____ However, she dropped out before graduating because her acting career was beginning to take off. She appeared in many films throughout the 1990s, including Tarantino's 1994 masterpiece *Pulp Fiction* and the 1997 science fiction classic, *Gattaca*. Today, she continues to be a respected and successful actress and model.

Future in the past

I can use different structures to talk about the future in the past.

1 Choose the best future in the past expression in these sentences.

1 She **was to have started** / **would start** her new job last Monday, but she was ill.

2 Some of the fans started to leave because the match **was about to end** / **would end**.

3 Even though it was a brief trip, she **was remembering** / **would remember** it forever.

4 She **was being** / **would be** in town later that afternoon because she **was taking** / **would take** her dog to the vet's.

5 When he met Claire, he had no idea how important she **was being** / **was to be** in his life.

6 They met in 1987 and **were to remain** / **were going to remain** friends for more than twenty years.

2 Complete the sentences using future in the past expressions from exercise 1.

'I can't go to the cinema. I'm going out for dinner.'
She couldn't go to the cinema because she was going out for dinner.

1 'There's no time to argue. The train leaves in five minutes!'
There was no time to argue because _____

2 'I'm excited. I'm going to meet Prince William.'
She was excited because _____

3 'We must find our seats. The show starts in two minutes.'
They had to find their seats because _____

4 'I'm looking for a job. I'll have to pay my university fees.'
She was looking for a job because _____

5 'She's nervous. She's taking her driving test soon.'
She was nervous because _____

6 'I know I'll never forget this wonderful day.'
He knew _____

3 Rewrite the e-mail as part of a narrative in the past. Include future in the past where necessary.

3rd July

It's the first day of my gap year. I'm about to leave on a six-month trip around Europe. I'm going to spend the first month in Spain working at a holiday camp and the second month in France on a language course. After that, I'll decide where to go next! I won't get another chance to go travelling for a while, so I'm really going to make the most of the experience. I'll definitely have some interesting stories to tell at the end of it!
love
Connor

It was 3rd July, and the first day of Connor's gap year. He was about to _____

4 Invent excuses to complete these sentences.

1 I was about to invite you to my birthday party but _____

2 I was going to hand in my homework on time but _____

3 I was planning to work harder this year but _____

Job interview

I can ask and answer questions in a job interview.

1 Complete this extract from an interview with questions a–f

a How long have you been in your current job?

b So why do you want to come and work here?

c What would you say your main qualities are as an employee?

d Would you be interested in going full-time at a later date?

e What do you enjoy most about your work?

f Do you realise that this is a part-time position?

Interviewer	¹_____
Alice	I'm honest, hardworking – and I'm a self-starter, too.
Interviewer	Good! We like self-starters in this company. ²_____
Alice	I'll have been there three years exactly next month.
Interviewer	³_____
Alice	Lots of things, really. But I suppose the best thing is working as part of a team. And also, dealing with the public – I really like that.
Interviewer	⁴_____
Alice	I just think it's the right time in my career for a new challenge.
Interviewer	I see. ⁵_____
Alice	Yes, I do. I'm planning to start a degree course with the Open University, so I need time for that.
Interviewer	I understand. ⁶_____
Alice	Perhaps. I hadn't really thought about it.

2 🎧 16 Listen to the whole interview and check your answers to exercise 1. What other two questions does the interviewer ask?

1 _____

_____

2 _____

_____

3 🎧 16 Listen again. Complete the phrases used at the beginning and end of the interview. Who says them? Write A (Alice) or I (Interviewer).

1 I'd like to _____ myself. _____

2 Pleased to _____ you. _____

3 I'd like to start by talking about your _____ . _____

4 Well, thanks for _____ in. _____

5 We'll be in _____ very soon. _____

6 I look forward to _____ from you. _____

4 Read the job advertisements. Which job was Alice being interviewed for? How do you know?

The National Portrait Gallery

is looking for a part-time marketing executive to join their busy promotional team. Experience of similar work is essential, as is a positive attitude. Salary negotiable, depending on qualifications.

THE BBC

is looking for a trainee producer to work in its Manchester studios. No experience required, but candidates must demonstrate enthusiasm and the ability to learn. An interest in current affairs and / or the arts is essential. Starting salary: £24,500 for a 35-hour week.

Hermes is looking for a senior retail assistant to join a friendly and effective team at its internationally renowned store in Knightsbridge, London. Great people skills are essential, and knowledge of other languages would be a distinct advantage. Salary dependent on age and experience.

It must have been _____

because _____

5 Imagine that you are being interviewed for one of the other jobs in exercise 4. Write three questions for the interviewer and appropriate answers for yourself. Choose expressions from exercise 3 to begin and end the interview.

_____

_____

_____

_____

_____

_____

_____

_____

_____

_____

_____

_____

Letter of application

*I can write a letter applying
for a place on a course.*

Preparation

1 Match the missing parts of the letter (1–7) with their correct position (a–h).

1 12ᵗʰ May 2009
2 M J Porter
3 112 Mill Street
   Milton Keynes
   MK12 7FG
4 Mark Porter
5 Trinity College
   Broad Street
   Oxford
   OX1 3BH
6 Dear Sir or Madam
7 Yours faithfully

ⓑ ☐   ☐ ⓐ

ⓒ ☐

ⓓ ☐

I am writing to apply for a place on your summer school course entitled The Great Romantic Poets, which I saw advertised on the Internet.
I am 19 years old and a first-year English student at the University of Buckingham. I am a Canadian national and have a two-year visa allowing me to study in the UK. I am particularly interested in your summer school for two reasons. Firstly, I intend to specialise in the Romantic Period next academic year. And secondly, I am keen to attend as many courses as possible during my relatively short time in this country.
I have two queries about the course. Firstly, could you tell me whether non-residential places are available? I have friends in Oxford with whom I could stay. Also, I would be grateful if you could let me know whether you envisage running a similar course at any other time of year.
I enclose my CV which includes details of my academic qualifications to date, as well as a personal profile. I look forward to hearing from you at your earliest convenience.

ⓔ ☐

ⓕ ☐

ⓖ ☐

---

2 Which eight of the highlighted words and phrases in the letter are quite formal English?

_____   _____

_____   _____

_____   _____

_____   _____

3 Complete this paragraph plan for the letter in exercise 1. Use the phrases in the box.

Personal information   Questions   Reason for writing Request for a reply

Paragraph 1: _____
Paragraph 2: _____
Paragraph 3: _____
Paragraph 4: _____

4 Read the advertisement and the task below. Plan your letter following the paragraph plan in exercise 3. Decide what two questions to ask.

Brit School Summer Course

We are offering two three-week courses during the summer vacation to allow students from all the over the world to sample the unique 'Brit School' experience. Find out why the school has produced some of the best-known and successful pop acts of the last ten years. Places are strictly limited, so apply early with full CV and covering letter explaining why you should be accepted onto the course.

Write to: Henry Grouse, Summer School Co-ordinator, The Brit School, PO Box 455, London

You have seen this advertisement online. Write a letter applying for a place on the course. Write 200–250 words.

5 Write your letter. Use the writing guide below to help you.

Writing Guide

1 Use the correct layout for a formal letter (see exercise 1).
2 Use appropriate formal language. Avoid slang or colloquial expressions. Use full forms rather than contractions.
3 Remember to sound as enthusiastic as possible about the course you are applying for.

CHECKLIST

Have you:
- followed the paragraph plan?
- included two queries in your letter?
- checked your work for mistakes?

A VOCABULARY
Space

I can talk about space exploration.

1 Read the clues and do the crossword.

Down

1 a group of stars that forms a shape in the sky
2 a tiny planet
3 the part of a rocket that the astronauts travel in
4 a large rock from space that makes a bright line in the sky as it enters the Earth's atmosphere
6 a large hole in the ground (e.g. caused by a meteorite, a bomb or a volcano)

Across

5 a scientist who studies the planets, stars, etc.
6 a huge piece of ice that orbits the sun, and looks like a bright star with a tail
7 the force that pulls things towards large objects like planets and the sun
8 an enormous system of stars in outer space
9 a very bright, exploding star

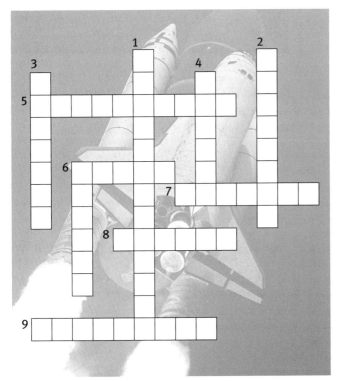

2 Complete the text with the words in the box. Change the verbs if necessary.

astronauts	atmosphere	crew	launch (v)
mission	mission control	orbit (n)	orbit (v)
re-enter	satellite	space shuttle (x2)	Space Station

Space disasters

On January 28, 1986, the [1]_____ Challenger was [2]_____ with a [3]_____ of seven on board. Its [4]_____ was to carry a [5]_____ that would [6]_____ the Earth. But just 73 seconds after blast off, it lost contact with [7]_____ and exploded, killing all seven [8]_____.
On 1st February 2003, the [9]_____ Columbia disintegrated as it [10]_____ the Earth's [11]_____. It was returning from the International [12]_____, which is in [13]_____ around the Earth.

●●●●● Extension: Space travel

3 Complete the compound nouns with the words in the box. (Some are two-word compounds, some are single-word compounds.)

craft	down	giant	hole	star	system	Way	year

a light _____
b black _____
c solar _____
d shooting _____
e red _____
f the Milky _____
g space _____
h touch _____

●●●●●● CHALLENGE! ●●●●●●

Try the space quiz. The answers are below.

1 Which astronomer first demonstrated that the sun, not the Earth, was at the centre of the Solar System?
   A Copernicus **B** Galileo **C** Halley
2 What is the 'Great Bear'?
   A a supernova **B** a star **C** a constellation
3 What did Sir Isaac Newton discover?
   A gravity **B** Pluto **C** black holes
4 According to astronomers, about how old is the universe?
   A 7 billion years **B** 14 billion years **C** 21 billion years
5 Travelling in a modern spacecraft, how far could you get in three years?
   A to the nearest star **B** to Pluto **C** to Saturn

1A 2C 3A 4B 5C

I can identify and use different forms of the passive.

1 Choose the correct form: passive infinitive or passive *-ing* form.

1 Jason doesn't mind **to be teased** / **being teased**.
2 I would like **to be invited** / **being invited** to Sue's party.
3 Imagine **to be followed** / **being followed** everywhere by the paparazzi.
4 I'll never forget **to be blamed** / **being blamed** at school for something I didn't do.
5 Harry begged **to be allowed** / **being allowed** to stay out late.
6 I didn't expect **to be made** / **being made** to wait for days for a doctor's appointment.
7 You risk **to be mugged** / **being mugged** if you walk home late at night in that part of town.
8 I remember **to be surprised** / **being surprised** by the news.

2 Complete the sentences with an appropriate passive form of the verbs in brackets.

1 By next Friday all the invitations _____ (send out).
2 The joyriders who _____ (arrest) by the police this morning were in a car that _____ (report) missing last night.
3 I had a feeling that I _____ (follow).
4 '_____ these windows _____ (clean)?' 'No, not yet.'
5 Right now the church _____ (renovate), so you can't go inside.
6 At the end of the training course, the astronauts _____ (choose) for the next space mission.

3 Make the active sentences passive.

1 You can find the address on our website.
_____

2 They shouldn't send shoplifters to prison.
_____

3 They must have lost my letter in the post.
_____

4 They might have built this church in the 10th century.
_____

5 They need to update the database.
_____

6 They can't have locked the door because someone had stolen the key.
_____
_____

4 Complete the texts with an appropriate passive form. Sometimes more than one answer is correct.

The planet Venus [1]_____ (name) after a Greek Goddess. Venus is approximately the same size as Earth and [2]_____ often _____ (call) Earth's sister planet. Because Venus is the only planet [3]_____ (give) a female name, it [4]_____ (decide) that most of the features on Venus should [5]_____ (name) after women.

Beagle 2 [6]_____ (built) by the European Space Agency in 2003 to explore the surface of Mars. Having [7]_____ (launch) from Kazakhstan, it reached Mars on Christmas Day 2003, but a few hours later, contact [8]_____ (lose). It might [9]_____ (damage) during its descent through the Martian atmosphere, but its exact fate may never [10]_____ (know).

●●●●●● **CHALLENGE!** ●●●●●●

Find out about another event in the history of space exploration and write about it. Use the ideas to help you.
• launched when / where?
• purpose of the mission?
• was it successful?

_____
_____
_____
_____
_____
_____
_____

Extra Practice

1 Complete the sentences with the words in the box.

adapted	broadcast	captured	fictional
fled	news bulletin	scandal	

1 Did you hear the latest _____ on the radio?
2 Dan Brown's novel, *The Da Vinci Code* was _____ for the cinema in 2005.
3 The *Harry Potter* books have _____ the imagination of teenagers all over the world.
4 *The War of the Worlds* radio programme caused a national _____ in 1938 because many of the listeners didn't realise that the events were _____.
5 The Wimbledon final was _____ live to millions of home around the world.
6 Many people have _____ from persecution in Darfur.

2 Quickly read the text and find:

1 Asimov's date and place of birth: _____
2 His age when he wrote his first story: _____
3 The year he died: _____

3 Complete the text with appropriate words.

4 Are the sentences true or false? Write T or F.

1 Asimov wrote more books than most 20th century writers. ____
2 He spoke three languages fluently. ____
3 His parents expected him to read the magazines that were sold in the family shop. ____
4 His first story was an instant success. ____
5 One of his stories in particular was much admired by other American science fiction writers. ____
6 He taught at a university before taking up writing full time. ____
7 He died of AIDS contracted from a blood transfusion. ____

Write about a writer who you admire. Include information about:
• nationality, date of birth
• type of books he/she wrote/writes
• other interesting events and facts

_____
_____
_____
_____

Isaac Asimov

Isaac Asimov is [1]_____ of the most successful and prolific science-fiction writers of the 20th century. He wrote or edited more than 500 books, the most famous of [2]_____ are the *Foundation* series and the *Robot* series.

Asimov was born Isaak Judah Ozimov in 1920, near Smolensk. In 1923 the family emigrated to the USA, settled in Brooklyn, New York, and changed the family name [3]_____ Azimov. Azimov spoke Yiddish and English at home with his family and so never learned more [4]_____ a little Russian. By the age of five he was a keen reader. His parents owned a series of sweet shops and the whole family was expected [5]_____ work in them. Azimov became fascinated with the science fiction magazines that [6]_____ sold in the family shops, and began reading them. When he was eleven he began to write his own stories, and by the age [7]_____ nineteen, he was selling them to the science fiction magazines. His first publication was *Marooned Off Vesta*, which was printed in the Amazing Stories magazine. But it was with his 32nd story, *Nightfall*, in 1941 that Asimov became really famous. The story is set on a planet [8]_____ night falls only once every 2049 years. In 1964 *Nightfall* was voted the best short science fiction story ever written [9]_____ the Science Fiction Writers of America. Many science fiction fans still agree with this verdict. [10]_____ leaving school, Azimov studied chemistry at Columbia University and went [11]_____ to become a professor at the Boston University School of Medicine. However, in [12]_____ 1950s he became a full-time writer. Asimov died on 6th April 1992. Ten years after his death, his wife revealed [13]_____ his death had been caused by AIDS. He had contracted HIV from a blood transfusion received during a heart bypass operation in December 1983.

Space tourism

I can understand and react to an article about space tourism.

Revision: Student's Book page 106–107

1 Complete the sentences with the phrasal verbs in the box. Use the correct tense and form.

check over	creep up	go through	head out
keep out	put on	slow down	start up	take in

1 The car _____ as it approached the traffic lights.
2 Last year house prices dropped, but they are gradually _____ again.
3 When you have finished your essay, _____ it _____ for mistakes.
4 There was a huge roar as the engines of the rocket _____ .
5 The ship left the harbour and _____ to sea.
6 We stopped at the top of the hill to _____ the wonderful views.
7 Can I _____ my lines with you before the dress rehearsal of the play?
8 The astronaut _____ her space suit before climbing into the capsule.
9 I don't want the cats in here. Can you close the door to _____ them _____ ?

2 Read the text, ignoring the gaps. Find out:

1 when the Galactic Suite will open

_____

2 the dimensions of the pods that guests will stay in

_____

3 how the guests will get to and from the Suite

_____

4 how many pods the architects plan to build

_____

5 which room caused the designers the most problems

_____

6 how much it will cost to stay in the Suite for three days

_____

7 which planet the company next intends to send holidaymakers to

_____

3 Match sentences A–H with gaps 1–7. There is one sentence that you do not need.

A There will be special rooms in which bubbles of water will float around.
B That's why the shuttle rocket will remain fixed to the space hotel, so guests know they can get home again.
C Furthermore, the Galactic Suite is fully booked for the next three years.
D For you will soon be able to have a holiday experience that is out of this world – literally.
E From your room you will enjoy the amazing sight of 15 different sunrises every day as you orbit the Earth every 80 minutes.
F However, it only sees this project as a first step.
G As usual, you need to be rich to travel in style.
H When they get tired of doing this, they will have great fun trying to stick to the walls in their Velcro suits, so that they can eat, sleep or simply admire the view from their enormous window.

4 Are the sentences true or false? Write T or F.

1 The Galactic Suite takes 1 hour and 20 minutes to orbit the Earth. _____
2 There is no single accommodation at the Galactic Suite. _____
3 The shuttle rocket will return to Earth after dropping off the guests. _____
4 There are some rooms in the Space Hotel that have gravity. _____
5 A complete package holiday to the Galactic Suite is about two months. _____
6 A Spanish company is behind the development of the Galactic Suite. _____

●●●●●● **CHALLENGE!** ●●●●●●

Would you like to have a holiday on the Galactic Suite? Why? / Why not?

_____
_____
_____
_____
_____
_____
_____
_____
_____

TAKE A SPACE BREAK

If you are getting tired of going to your relatives for a weekend away, or having the same old holidays in the same old places, and if you are feeling especially brave and adventurous, then we suggest that you start saving your money now. ¹_____

Make your booking now for a few days in the Galactic Suite, the perfect way to broaden your horizons – in outer space. You will be able to stay in one of its amazing zero-gravity rooms, each one with spectacular views of planet Earth! ²_____

The opening of the Galactic Suite is planned for 2012, and at first there will only be room for six guests at a time. Each of the three double bedrooms is in the shape of a pod, seven metres long and four metres high. The three pods will be joined together at one end to the main hotel, looking like a cluster of molecules. Each room will have almost no furniture, as guests will be floating around in zero gravity. ³_____

The Galactic Suite is being designed by a group of architects in Barcelona. Each pod is small enough to be transported inside a US space shuttle which will put them into space. Once the hotel is ready, the shuttle will also carry the guests to and from their destination, and will be 'parked' outside during their stay. Xavier Claramunt, one of the directors of the company working on the project, said, 'There is fear associated with going into space. ⁴_____ ' Eventually, the Spanish architects plan to have up to 22 pods clustered round a communal centre.

Mr Claramunt admitted that there have been several design challenges during the project, the biggest of which has been how to design the bathrooms for zero gravity. 'How to accommodate the more intimate activities of the guests is not easy,' he added. But the designers may have solved the issue of how to take a shower in weightlessness. ⁵_____ You will have to catch your bath!

Orbiting Earth won't be a holiday option for the average-income family, however. ⁶_____ A three-day stay is expected to cost £2 million. This price also includes eight weeks of intensive training at a sophisticated space camp in the Caribbean. Mr Claramunt explained, 'We have calculated that there are 40,000 people in the world who could afford to stay at the hotel.'

The Galactic Suite is a £1.5 billion project backed by a US company who are planning to make science fiction a reality. ⁷_____ The company is intent on colonising Mars. Anybody fancy a holiday on the Red Planet in 2020?

Passive: advanced structures

I can use advanced passive structures.

1 Complete the text with passive forms.

Hundreds of UFO sightings [1]_____
(report) every year but the most famous UFO story is
probably the 'Roswell incident' which took place in
1947. It [2]_____ (allege) at the time that
an alien spacecraft had crashed in the desert in New
Mexico. Shortly after, a number of alien bodies
[3]_____ (rumour) to have been removed
from the wreckage by US soldiers. It [4]_____
(not know) where the bodies [5]_____ (take).
For many years these reports [6]_____ (deny)
by military sources, who maintained that what
[7]_____ (recover) was a top-secret
research balloon, that had crashed. Finally, in 1997
the military admitted that bodies [8]_____ indeed
_____ (take) from the wreckage, but that
they were test-flight dummies that [9]_____
(drop) from high altitude as part of an experiment.
However, many people dismiss this version of events.
Since 1947 numerous books [10]_____
(write) on the incident, but the truth still remains
shrouded in mystery.

2 Rewrite the sentences so that they have the same meaning.
Use a different passive construction.

1 It is thought that the satellite burned up in the atmosphere.
   The satellite is _____

2 It is alleged that he murdered his wife.
   He _____

3 It is said that he moved to the USA.
   _____

4 It is believed that terrorists planted the bomb.
   _____

5 It is now known that five people died in the accident.
   _____

6 It is reported that the car was stolen last night.
   _____

3 Rewrite the sentences using *it* + passive, or passive + *to do
/ to have done*.

1 People say that prices will go up next year.
   It is said that prices will go up next year.

2 People once thought that the Earth was flat.
   _____

3 People think that we will one day colonise the moon.
   _____

4 They believe the thief stole all the paintings.
   _____

5 People suspected that the woman was a witch.
   _____

6 They claim that Henry wasn't who he said he was.
   _____

7 They say that the weather is going to improve.
   _____

8 People consider him to be a very rich man.
   _____

4 Rewrite the sentences so that they have the same meaning.
Use the passive and start with the word(s) given.

1 They gave the teacher a present at the end of the year.
   The teacher _____

2 They don't serve alcohol to people under 18.
   Alcohol _____

3 Nobody has taught him good manners.
   He _____

4 My boss promised me a big pay rise.
   I _____

5 They gave me ten minutes to make up my mind.
   I _____

6 They didn't offer the job to Martin.
   The job _____

7 They gave a prize to the cleverest student.
   A prize _____

8 £100 is owed to Harry by the bank.
   Harry _____

Extra Practice

1 Complete the phrases using the words in the box.

> accept alter deny far having maintain
> nevertheless opinion own people personally
> true way would

1 Admittedly, ... ☐
2 As _____ as I'm concerned ... ☐
3 But _____ said that, I still think that ... ☐
4 But I _____ still say that ... ☐
5 However, this doesn't _____ my view that ... ☐
6 I wouldn't _____ that ... ☐
7 In my _____ ... ☐
8 It is _____ that ... ☐
9 My _____ view is that ... ☐
10 _____, I still believe that ... ☐
11 Of course, we have to _____ that ... ☐
12 Others _____ that ... ☐
13 _____, I believe that ... ☐
14 Some _____ think that ... ☐
15 The _____ I look at it, ... ☐

2 Put the phrases into three groups. Write a, b, c or d next to the phrases.

a outlining the issue
b making a point
c acknowledging an opposing point
d re-stating your original point

3 🎧 17 Read the exam question below and listen to the presentations. Are the sentences true or false?

Do you think that life exists on other planets in our galaxy?
Do you think we will ever make contact with alien life forms?

1 Both speakers believe that life must exist on other planets. ____
2 Neither speaker believes that we will ever make contact with alien life forms. ____

4 🎧 17 Listen again. Put the sentences in the order that you hear them.

a Personally, I believe that ... ☐
b In my view ... ☐
c However, this doesn't alter my view that ... ☐
d Of course, we have to accept that ... ☐
e Some people argue that ... ☐
f I would say that ... ☐
g Let's be honest, ... ☐
h On balance, if you ask me, I'd say that ... ☐

5 Write a brief presentation (about 100 words) of your opinions on the exam question below. Use the ideas below to help you. Follow the plan in exercise 2, and give examples to back up the points you make.

Do you think it might one day be necessary to colonise the moon or other planets in our solar system? Do you think it would be possible or desirable?

> **Why it might be necessary/desirable:**
> • Earth's population is rapidly increasing
> • global warming and climate change
> • space tourism
> • mankind's drive to explore and seek adventure
>
> **Why it might not be possible/desirable:**
> • should solve the problems on Earth
> • population control
> • inhospitable environment on other planets
> • breathable atmosphere
> • gravity
> • the danger of accidents
> • quality of life?

WRITING
Narrative

I can write a descriptive story.

Preparation

1 Rewrite the sentences using the word given.

   1 Many galaxies are shaped like discs. (shape)

       _____

   2 The sky was the colour of slate. (coloured)

       _____

   3 The alien was as big as a small house. (size)

       _____

   4 You can see the wood from the road. (visible)

       _____

   5 There's a house at the end of this lane. (stands)

       _____

2 Combine the pairs of sentences into a single sentence. Use each structure (a–d) once.

a *after* + *-ing*	**b** *having* + past participle
c a present participle	**d** *as* + past simple

   1 They left Italy. Then they drove to Spain.

       _____

   2 Jack came into the room. At the same time, he tripped on the rug.

       _____

   3 She knocked on the door. She went in.

       _____

   4 I left the house. At the same time, it started to rain.

       _____

3 Write the story told in the pictures, or invent one of your own. Use the writing guide to help you.

Writing Guide

1 Set the scene and introduce the main character(s).
2 Describe the problem that the characters face.
3 Describe how the problem is solved.
4 Write the ending: what happened? How did people feel?

> ### CHECKLIST
>
> **Have you:**
> * followed the writing guide?
> * used sequencing clauses?
> * used a variety of expressions to make your descriptions more interesting and vivid?

 Extra Practice

EXAM TASK – Reading

Read the text below and for questions 1–6 choose the answer A, B, C or D that fits best according to the text.

In Egyptian mythology, Apophis was the ancient spirit of evil and destruction. So it seemed a fitting name for a 390-metre wide asteroid that is potentially on a collision course with our planet. NASA has estimated that an impact from Apophis, which has an outside chance of hitting the Earth in 2036, would release more than 100,000 times the energy released in the nuclear blast over Hiroshima. Thousands of square kilometres would be directly affected by the blast but the whole of the Earth would see the effects of the dust released into the atmosphere.

Apophis had been intermittently tracked since its discovery in June 2004 but, in December, it started causing serious concern. Projecting the orbit of the asteroid into the future, astronomers calculated that the odds of it hitting the Earth were alarming. As more observations came in, the odds got higher. The asteroid was placed at four out of ten on the Torino scale – a measure of the threat posed by a near-Earth object, where 10 is a certain collision. This was the highest of any asteroid in recorded history.

Alan Fitzsimmons, an astronomer from Queen's University Belfast, said: 'When it does pass close to us in April 2029, the Earth will deflect it and change its orbit. There's a small possibility that if it passes through a particular point in space, the so-called keyhole, the Earth's gravity will change things so that when it comes back around again in 2036, it will collide with us.' The chance of Apophis passing through the keyhole, a 600-metre patch of space, is 1 in 5,500 based on current information.

There is no shortage of ideas on how to deflect the asteroid. No technology has been left unconsidered, even potentially dangerous ideas such as nuclear powered spacecraft. The favoured method is also potentially the easiest – throwing a spacecraft at an asteroid to change its direction. The European Space Agency plans to test this idea with its Don Quixote mission, where two satellites will be sent to an asteroid. One of them, Hidalgo, will collide with the asteroid at high speed while the other, Sancho, will measure the change in the object's orbit. Decisions on the actual design of these probes will be made in the coming months, with the launch expected some time in the next decade. One idea that seems to have no support from astronomers is the use of explosives.

In September, scientists at Strathclyde and Glasgow universities began computer simulations to work out the feasibility of changing the directions of asteroids on a collision course for Earth. In spring next year, there will be another opportunity for radar observations of Apophis that will help astronomers work out possible future orbits of the asteroid more accurately.

If, at that stage, they cannot rule out an impact with Earth in 2036, the next chance to make better observations will not be until 2013. NASA has argued that a final decision on what to do about Apophis will have to be made next spring.

'It may be a decision in 2013 whether or not to go ahead with a full-blown mitigation mission, but we need to start planning it before 2013,' said Prof Fitzsimmons. In 2029, astronomers will know for sure if Apophis will pose a threat in 2036. If the worst-case scenarios turn out to be true and the Earth is not prepared, it will be too late.

1 Apophis
  A has the potential to destroy the whole of the Earth.
  B may cause damage comparable to that of a nuclear bomb.
  C is larger than any asteroid recorded by NASA so far.
  D has been given a name to match the threat it represents.

2 When Apophis was discovered, scientists
  A predicted the orbit it will make in the future.
  B immediately realised how dangerous it was.
  C decided they would never let it out of sight.
  D invented a scale to measure the threat it posed.

3 According to Professor Alan Fitzsimmons
  A it's probable Apophis won't come near the Earth in 2029.
  B passing through the keyhole may be a decisive factor.
  C in 2029, the asteroid may change the Earth's gravity.
  D the chance of Apophis avoiding the Earth is 1 in 5,500.

4 Scientists believe that
  A we have no effective technology now to solve the problem.
  B the best way to deal with the asteroid would be to blow it up.
  C a controlled collision could stop Apophis from hitting the Earth.
  D nuclear powered spacecraft is too difficult a solution.

5 Hidalgo and Sancho
  A will be sent to change the direction of Apophis.
  B will be sent into space within the next ten years.
  C are expected to carry out some measurements in Apophis.
  D will be sent to blow up an asteroid.

6 Scientists know that
  A 2013 will be too late to start planning a mitigation mission.
  B they will send a mitigation mission in 2013.
  C they have to begin planning a mitigation mission in 2013.
  D the last moment to send a mitigation mission will be 2029.

EXAM TASK – Use of English

Complete the text with suitable words. Use one word only in each gap.

Here's a conversation worth talking [1]_____: a mother dolphin chats with her baby...over the telephone! [2]_____ special call was made in an aquarium in Hawaii, where the mother and her two-year-old calf swam in separate tanks connected by a special underwater audio link. The two dolphins began squawking and chirping to each other – distinctive dolphin chatter.

'It seemed clear that they knew [3]_____ they were talking with,' says Don White, whose Project Delphis ran the experiment. 'Information was passing back and forth pretty quickly.' But what did they say? That's what scientists are trying to find [4]_____ by studying wild and captive dolphins all over the world to decipher their secret language. They haven't completely cracked the code yet, but they're listening...and learning.

Scientists think dolphins 'talk' about everything from basic facts like their age to their emotional state. They may be saying things [5]_____ 'there are some good fish over here,' or 'watch out [6]_____ that shark because he is hunting'.

When the going gets tough, for instance, some dolphins call [7]_____ backup. After being bullied [8]_____ a duo of bottlenose dolphins, one spotted dolphin returned to the scene the next day with a few pals to chase and harass one of the bully bottlenose dolphins. 'It's as [9]_____ the spotted dolphin communicated to his buddies that he needed their help, then led them in search [10]_____ this guy,' says Herzing, who cannot forget watching the scuffle.

EXAM TASK – Listening

🎧18　**Read the statements. Then listen to the recording and choose the best way to finish each statement.**

1　Christine's mum
　A　is not a sports person.
　B　does the same sport as Christine.
　C　has never worked.

2　Ella
　A　shares the same personality as her mum.
　B　has inherited a love of craftwork.
　C　is a member of her mum's handball team.

3　Penny
　A　wants to become a physician.
　B　spends all her time with her mum.
　C　is an only child.

EXAM TASK – Writing

You successfully graduated from secondary school yesterday. Write a short note (100–120 words) to your friends announcing this news and invite them to a party you plan to give.

In your note, you should:
- say when the party will be given
- give directions to the party
- tell your friends what to bring (e.g. food, drinks)
- ask them to reply by a certain date

Write your note in the appropriate style and format.

PREPARATION: Speaking

Use the Functions Bank on page 102 to help you.

EXAM TASK – Speaking

Part 3 – Sustained long turn

You will be asked to talk about your country and its culture.

Consider the following points:
- Your native town
- Historical issues
- Your country as a tourist destination (places of interest to recommend)
- Public holidays in your country
- National customs
- Other

Part 4 – Role play

Work in pairs and role-play the following situation.

Role 1 (You are a student)
You are talking to the parent of your close friend who has some problems at school. His/her grades have not been very good recently and s/he has also been playing truant. Try to defend him/her and explain his/her behaviour without saying too much about your friend's secrets.

Role 2 (You are a parent)
You are talking to a close friend of your son/daughter who has some problems at school. His/her grades have not been very good recently and s/he has also been playing truant. You are very unhappy about it and believe that your child spends too much time with his/her friends. Try to find out what is happening.

You may use these ideas:
- Unpopular/problematic subject/s
- A youth gang
- Bullying
- Addiction (drugs, alcohol, etc.)
- Other

When you have finished, change roles and practise again.

READING

Read the article about a film entitled *Báthory* and complete the sentences (1–10). Use a suitable word or words (maximum three) from the text so that the sentences correspond to what the article says. The sentences do not follow the same order as the information appears in the text.

History's judgment of Elizabeth Báthory appeared unanimous – until now.

According to legend, as well as several bestsellers, the 16th century Hungarian noblewoman who ruled over a vast kingdom from her castle above the village of Čachtice in present-day Slovakia became so obsessed with attaining eternal youth she slaughtered more than 600 young girls to bathe in their blood.

But in Báthory, Slovak director Juraj Jakubisko looks behind the myths and suggests the 'Bloody Countess' was actually a victim of a smear campaign rooted in political and ethnic strife.

The film, which is the 69-year-old director's first in English, had a €11.5-million budget, making it the most expensive Central European movie ever made. Since wrapping in 2006, it has created a buzz with showings at film festivals in Los Angeles and Berlin.

'In today's digital age, fewer European feature film projects embrace major international stories on such a grand scale,' Mike Downey, a co-producer from the UK-based Film and Music Entertainment production company, said about the film for *Variety*. 'Juraj Jakubisko is a master of cinematic style, and we invested in his vision because it is a film of ambition, scope and scale destined for worldwide theatrical release.'

Jakubisko began the film's long evolution by writing the screenplay, which was translated into English before being sent to screenwriter John Paul Chapple. 'The version of the script I received was immensely long, around 200 pages,' Chapple told *The Slovak Spectator*. 'I worked on shaping it more to western standards, which meant cutting down the amount of description and remodelling the dialogue from a literary style into lines that were more speakable and actable. Jakubisko's translators helped me the whole time to make sure I kept faithful to the original intent.'

'There are so many legends about her which just aren't true,' Jakubisko told Czech Radio in May. 'The idea that she bathed in the blood of young girls to retain her eternal youth for example. You can't bathe in blood because blood clots. And even historians are divided about her legacy because for the older generation, Elizabeth Báthory was this Hungarian countess who murdered Slovak girls.

'There is a lot of folklore and Báthory is a strong, warrior-like heroine who has a duty to her country, which stretched from the borders of Moravia all the way to the Adriatic Sea, and she basically had to do it single-handedly.'

'If Báthory combines critical and commercial success it could well change the profile of Slovak film by making it known internationally,' Peter Hames, an expert on Central European film and author of *The Czechoslovak New Wave*, told *The Slovak Spectator*. 'For the same reasons, it would be likely to encourage other large budget films in the English language, since success is always followed by imitation.'

1 The story is set in the _____ .
2 Báthory is said to have wanted to succeed in staying _____ for ever.
3 Báthory was also known under the nickname of the _____ .
4 According to Jakubisko, Báthory was a(n) _____ of political disagreements.
5 They have never made such a costly film in _____ before.
6 Jakubisko's directing skills mean that the film will be distributed around the _____ .
7 The original script was rewritten to better suit _____ .
8 The amount of _____ in the original script was reduced.
9 _____ disagree about the role Báthory played in the past.
10 Báthory had moral and legal responsibility for _____ .

USE OF ENGLISH

1 **Complete the text with suitable words. Use one word only in each gap.**

SLEEPING HABITS

The analysis published in October 2006 in *Nature* shows that meat-eating species sleep the most and grazing animals the [1]_____ . Sleep amounts range from 20 hours in the little brown bat to only two hours in the horse. Animals that have less sleep do not appear to make [2]_____ for this by sleeping more deeply.

The analysis concludes that sleep functions to keep animals safe by restricting waking to the hours when an animal is most likely to be successful [3]_____ finding food and avoiding danger.

Human sleep follows the rules that determine sleep time in other animals. Humans sleep somewhat less [4]_____ animals with similar physiological features, suggesting that we may [5]_____ evolved to have more waking hours in order to better compete with other humans.

Some animals can go without sleep for long periods of time with [6]_____ ill effects, whereas lack of sleep in [7]_____ can be lethal. [8]_____ explains [9]_____ some animals can survive and reproduce optimally [10]_____ though they are only awake for a few hours and eat very little, whereas others need to eat all day and must have reduced sleep time.

2 Complete the text with the correct form of the words in brackets.

A green consultant is a researcher, facilitator, [1]_____ (ADVISE), and educator. A good green building consultant has an understanding of issues, products and technologies relating to [2]_____ (SUSTAIN) sites, energy, water, indoor air quality, materials and construction practices. We help owners, architects and other design and construction professionals who are not as familiar with these issues to [3]_____ (SHORT) the time it would take to learn it all. We help them design and construct buildings in a cost-effective and more [4]_____ (ENVIRONMENT) responsible way.

The most difficult thing is convincing people to do things [5]_____ (DIFFERENT). Design professionals and construction contractors usually want to do things the way they have done them in the past because it's less [6]_____ (RISK) and they don't have to spend any time figuring out how to do something new.

Another problem to be dealt with are buildings which are one of the biggest [7]_____ (CONTRIBUTE) to global [8]_____ (WARM) due to their typically [9]_____ (EFFICIENT) energy use. Buildings account for 39% of total energy use, 68% of total electricity [10]_____ (CONSUME) and 38% of the carbon dioxide emissions. When you understand that most people spend over 90% of their time indoors, this makes a lot of sense.

WRITING

1 You have decided to join the discussion in a local newspaper about banning smoking in public places. Write an essay of 210–230 words entitled *'Smoking in public places should be made illegal'* arguing your point of view.

2 Join the discussion in a local newspaper about the lifestyle of young people. Write an argumentative essay entitled *'Young people do not live healthily.'* Write 210–230 words arguing your point of view.

SPEAKING

TASK 1

Look at the pictures showing a scene from daily life in order to compare and contrast them.

These ideas may help you:
- Environment/ setting
- Architecture/ buildings
- Mood
- Advantages/ disadvantages of living there
- People
- Other

TASK 2

Read the quotation below and express your opinion on it.

These ideas may help you:
- Do you agree or disagree with the quotation? Why?
- Support your opinion with an example/your own experience.

'Knowledge rests not upon truth alone, but upon error also.' Carl Jung

TASK 3

You will be asked to talk about animal rights.

The following ideas may help you:
- National parks and protected landscape areas in your country and their importance
- Endangered species
- Violation of animal rights (zoos, experiments carried on animals, having pets)
- Your experience, e.g. visit to a zoo
- Other

TASK 4

Work in pairs and role-play the following situation.

Role 1 – You are finishing secondary school and have decided to take a gap year before you start studying at university. You are thinking about working as a volunteer somewhere in Africa or Australia where you could both work and study English. You could also work as a volunteer anywhere in Europe. All options are tempting and you cannot decide. Discuss this with your friend and ask him/her to give you some advice.

Role 2 – Your friend is finishing secondary school and has decided to take a gap year before s/he starts studying at university. S/he is thinking about working as a volunteer somewhere in Africa or Australia where s/he could both work and study English. S/he could also work as a volunteer anywhere in Europe. All options are tempting and s/he cannot decide. S/he wants you to give him/her some advice.

READING

Read the article about plastic shopping bags. Match each paragraph (A–E) to its summary (1–6). There is one number which you do not need to use.

Plastic shopping bags and the environment

A

It's easy to be green. Although we may be overwhelmed by the environmental catastrophes that seem to occur around us with alarming regularity, there is a simple way each and every person can make a difference. It doesn't involve travelling the world to clean up oil spills or standing in the path of bulldozers to prevent land clearing. It actually involves shopping …

B

The environmental issues associated with plastic shopping bags have featured in the news recently, following the apparent success of the plastic bag tax in Ireland in reducing the number of plastic shopping bags that are used in that country. While this approach has also been suggested for addressing the problem in other countries, governments still tend to examine a number of options before deciding on a management plan. In the meantime, the best thing we can do for the environment is simply reuse, or better yet, refuse a plastic bag when we go shopping. Easy!

C

Plastic shopping bags have a surprisingly significant environmental impact for something so seemingly innocuous. As well as being an eyesore, plastic shopping bags kill large numbers of wildlife each year. In the water, plastic bags can be mistaken for jellyfish by wildlife. This makes plastic bag pollution in marine environments particularly dangerous, as birds, whales, seals and turtles ingest the bags then die from intestinal blockages. Disturbingly, it is claimed that plastic bags are the most common man-made item seen by sailors at sea.

D

The biggest problem with plastic bags is that they do not readily break down in the environment, with estimates for the time it takes them to decompose ranging from 20 to 1,000 years. One of the disquieting facts stemming from this is that plastic bags can become serial killers. Once an animal that had ingested a plastic bag dies, it decays at a much faster rate than the bag. When the animal has decomposed, the bag is released back into the environment more or less intact, ready to be eaten by another misguided organism. The incredibly slow rate of decay of plastic bags also means that each bag we use compounds the problem, because the bags simply accumulate.

E

On top of the significant environmental costs, widespread use of plastic bags is also costly in terms of dollars and cents. Apart from the price of the bags themselves, which is four to six cents each, a great deal of money goes into collecting the bags (i.e. cleaning up!) once they've been discarded.

1 Plastic bags threaten not only natural environments but also urban ones.
2 Above all, bags are definitely not worth the money spent on them.
3 It is easy to get the wrong impression that plastic bags are underwater creatures.
4 Of great concern is the fact that a single bag can kill several living things.
5 Governmental policies on how to avoid using plastic bags vary from country to country.
6 You can help the situation and you don't need to be an eager environmentalist.

USE OF ENGLISH

1 Complete the extract with suitable words.

Lily sat down and looked at the child in front of her. He was small and thin and wore a jacket that was [1]_____ large for him. His eyes were half hidden [2]_____ a long messy fringe. Where had he come from? [3]_____ they had found him in the park, he had said nothing to [4]_____ at the police station. It was Lily's responsibility to question [5]_____ . She smiled gently. 'What's your name?' she asked. The boy looked at her across the table and said [6]_____ . He blinked. She [7]_____ see that he didn't understand. She tried again, [8]_____ time in French. The boy's expression did not change. He did not try to speak. Then she had an idea: [9]_____ if he could not hear her? Nobody had guessed that he [10]_____ be deaf. Lily smiled [11]_____ the boy again and waved. He looked back at her, puzzled. [12]_____ would not do. Lily picked up the phone and called for assistance.

2 Read the text and choose the correct form of the verbs (A–C).

One day, after school, one of the girls in my class said she
¹_____ me a new way to get home. She wasn't a nice girl, and I was a bit dubious about going with her... and to tell the truth, I was somewhat afraid of her because she was a bully. Anyway, Pat
²_____ me away from our normal route into the residential streets around the school. A few twists and turns, and ... I ³_____ . At that point, Pat said: 'I'm going to leave you here, you
⁴_____ home,' and then she ran.

Of course I tried to follow her, but she must
⁵_____ herself because when I turned the corner, she wasn't there. Being the brave, adventurous type of child, I only blubbered a little before trying
⁶_____ my way back. Naturally enough nothing was familiar. At some point Pat appeared again – she must ⁷_____ me, watching to see what I ⁸_____. I distinctly remember
⁹_____ her, 'I don't like you!' and then I marched off without looking back.

Luckily for me I eventually recognised a street that I passed on my usual way home – that was a huge relief. Perhaps Pat was just being mischievous and she
¹⁰_____ me there and gone home herself. This is what I'll never know. But I'm giving her the benefit of doubt because I'm a nice person.

1 **A** will show	**B** would show	**C** would have shown
2 **A** led	**B** has been leading	**C** would lead
3 **A** was losing	**B** would lose	**C** was lost
4 **A** will never get	**B** are never getting	**C** have never got
5 **A** hide	**B** have hidden	**C** be hiding
6 **A** find	**B** finding	**C** to find
7 **A** be following	**B** followed	**C** have been following
8 **A** would do	**B** had done	**C** did
9 **A** telling	**B** to tell	**C** have told
10 **A** hadn't left	**B** wouldn't have left	**C** didn't leave

WRITING

1 Your friends are animal lovers and you want to go for a trip together. Write a letter to them (210–230 words) in which you describe a place you would recommend for the trip.

2 Your friends love doing sports and you want to spend a weekend together with them. Write a letter to them (210–230 words) in which you describe a place you would recommend for the weekend.

In your letter include these points:
• how you found out about the place
• describe the place, its atmosphere and the animals you can see
• activities you can do there
• your opinion of the place

Write your letter in an appropriate style. Do not write any dates or addresses.

SPEAKING

TASK 1
These two pictures show people doing different kinds of painting. Compare and contrast them, say why the activity is important for these people and which of them you would prefer to do and why.

TASK 2
You will be asked to talk about reading books.

Consider the following points:
• The importance of reading
• Young people and literature. Reading books and watching films or television.
• The future of books
• Your favourite book

TASK 3
Work in pairs and role-play the following situation.

Role 1 – (You are a student.) After finishing secondary school you want to find a job in an English-speaking country and work and live there for at least a year. Your parents are against it and they want you to study at university. However, you do not want to study at the moment. Explain your reasons and try to persuade them.

Role 2 – (You are a parent.) After finishing secondary school your child wants to find a job in an English-speaking country and work and live there for at least a year. However, you believe it is a waste of time and want your child to study at university. Give your reasons and try to persuade him/her.

REVIEW 1 1–2

1 Complete the text with the correct words a–d.

Making Monet

John Myatt is a painter. He is not, he is the first to
¹_____, the world's finest artist. He is, however, quite
²_____ the world's finest forger. In 1998 John Myatt
was sentenced to a year in prison for his part in what
was described ³_____ the 20th-century's biggest
⁴_____ art fraud. For eight years, between 1986 and
1994, he and his London-based accomplice, John
Drewe, passed off over 200 works of art as ⁵_____
'found' pieces by surrealists, cubists, impressionists.
They sold, for tens of thousands of pounds, in
the ⁶_____ London auction houses, Christie's and
Sotheby's, and fooled Britain's two most prestigious
museums: the Victoria and Albert Museum and
the Tate Gallery. One 'Giacometti' was bought at
auction in New York ⁷_____ $300,000. Some say
the British market has never quite ⁸_____ from the
scandal. What Myatt is doing now, however, for up
to £5,000 a painting, is forging to order, entirely
legitimately. His 'genuine fakes' are painted in
⁹_____ house paint, and stamped as 'fake' on the
back, and his ¹⁰_____ versions of, say, Giacometti's
Seated Nude, or Matisse's The Pink Room, now
grace ski lodges in Aspen and villas in Tuscany.

1 **a** reveal	**b** admit	**c** disclose	**d** realise
2 **a** maybe	**b** perhaps	**c** eventually	**d** possibly
3 **a** as	**b** like	**c** for	**d** to
4 **a** new	**b** contemporary	**c** present	**d** recent
5 **a** true	**b** authentic	**c** genuine	**d** real
6 **a** major	**b** important	**c** significant	**d** chief
7 **a** at	**b** up to	**c** from	**d** for
8 **a** recuperated	**b** recovered	**c** rallied	**d** repaired
9 **a** typical	**b** ordinary	**c** usual	**d** routine
10 **a** perfect	**b** ultimate	**c** ideal	**d** exemplary

Mark | /10

2 In many lines in this letter between a British girl and her American penfriend there is one wrong word which should not be there. Find the wrong word, cross it out and write it at the end of the line. Some lines are correct. Tick ✓ the correct lines. There are two examples at the beginning.

31st July

Dear Jack

been	How are you? Sorry I haven't ~~been~~ written to
✓	you for ages, but I've been really busy
_____	recently. The last month I took my A level
_____	exams – they're the exams you take just
_____	before you will leave school. They were quite
_____	difficult but I did a lots of revision, so I think
_____	I did OK. I've applied to study economics
_____	here in Bristol.
_____	No sooner when had the exams finished
_____	than we went off on holiday to Menton. It's
_____	situated in the south-west of the France.
_____	We spent a week there then drove inland and
_____	stayed in the village of Sospel. The weather
_____	was great – it has only rained one day – and
_____	we had a fantastic time for swimming, and
_____	walking in the Mercantour National Park.
_____	So, now I'm back home. There's a little to do,
_____	but that suits me fine! Mum's been
_____	encouraging to me to get a summer job but
_____	I prefer it to just hang about with my friends,
_____	read books and watch TV.
_____	That's about all for now. Write soon and tell
_____	me your news.

Best wishes

Emily

Mark | /10

1 Complete the text with the correct form of the words in brackets.

It's a dog's life

Five puppies have been born in the world's first
¹_____ (CLONE) of a pet dog for a paying customer.
They are the ²_____ (GENE) doubles of a dog called
Booger, whose death from cancer two years ago left
his ³_____ (OWN) Bernann McKinney so upset that
she sold her house to raise the £25,000 needed to – in
her eyes – bring him back to life. Ms McKinney rescued
Booger from a dogs' home. He became an ⁴_____
(DISPENSE) part of her life after defending her and
saving her life when she was attacked by another
dog. Miss McKinney said, 'Booger was my partner and
my friend. The puppies are ⁵_____ (EXACT) the
same as their daddy.' RNL Bio, the Korean ⁶_____
(ORGANISE) that cloned the dogs, said the ⁷_____
(PROCEED) was so straightforward that it could clone
300 dogs a year for people whose pets had died. The
Booger puppies, who were born last week, have black
coats and identical white spots below their necks.
⁸_____ (SCIENCE) Lee Byeong-chun said all five
puppies were healthy, although there were slight
⁹_____ (VARY) in weight. A ¹⁰_____ (DELIGHT)
Ms McKinney said their birth had healed the pain of
Booger's death. 'It is a miracle for me because I was
able to smile again, laugh again and just feel alive
again,' she explained.

Mark   /10

2 Choose the best verb forms.

25th August

Dear Emily,

Thanks for your letter. I hope you ¹**could/managed to** pass
your A level exams. When ²**are you finding out/will you
find out** if you've got a place at college? We didn't have
any exams at the end of term, thank goodness. ³**I've been/
I'd been** offered a place at the University of Texas in
Austin to study law, providing ⁴**I get/I'll get** good grades
in my exams next May. I guess I'd better work harder this
year!

Your vacation sounded great. I ⁵**didn't do/haven't been
doing** much lately, but tomorrow I'm off on a camping
holiday in Florida. I don't particularly like camping but I
was persuaded to go by my friends. This time next week
⁶**I'll probably sit/I'll probably be sitting** in a tent in Florida
wishing I was back home. I hope I don't get bitten by the
mosquitoes! Anyway, ⁷**I'll send/I'd send** you a postcard.

As soon as ⁸**I return/I'll return** from Florida I'm starting
work in the local store. The pay isn't great but ⁹**I can/I'll be
able to** earn enough to pay back the money ¹⁰**I borrowed/
had borrowed** from my parents for the vacation.

I look forward to hearing from you again.

Best wishes

Jack

Mark   /10

1 Complete the text with the words in the box.

as	back	by	for	for	in	like	on
through	throughout						

The oldest newspaper in the world

¹_____ centuries, readers have thumbed ²_____ the pages of Sweden's *Post-och Inrikes Tidningar* newspaper. No longer. The world's oldest paper still ³_____ circulation has dropped its paper edition and now exists only in cyberspace. The newspaper, founded in 1645 ⁴_____ Sweden's Queen Kristina, became an Internet-only publication on 1st January. It's a fate that may await many of the world's most famous newspapers. 'We think it's a cultural disaster,' said Hans Holm, who served ⁵_____ the chief editor of Post-och Inrikes Tidningar for 20 years. 'It is sad when you have worked with it for so long and it has been around for so long.' ⁶_____ in the seventeenth century, Queen Kristina used the publication to keep her subjects informed of the affairs of state, and the first editions, which were more ⁷_____ leaflets, were carried by courier and put on notice boards in cities and towns ⁸_____ Sweden.

The paper edition was certainly no mass-market tabloid. ⁹_____ the contrary, it had a meagre circulation of only 1,000 or so, although the web-based version is expected to attract more readers. The newspaper is owned by the Swedish Academy, known ¹⁰_____ awarding the annual Nobel Prize in Literature. Despite its online transformation, *Post-och Inrikes Tidningar* remains Number 1 on a ranking of the oldest newspapers still in circulation.

Mark /10

2 Find and correct ten more mistakes in this letter.

1st December

Dear Jack,

_____ How are things with you? You said in your
you've been last letter that ⟨you been⟩ offered a place at
_____ the University of Texas. I suppose your
_____ exams are quite soon now, don't they?
_____ I hope that you enjoy yourself and that you
_____ don't have to working too hard this year.
_____ I got my A level exam results in August, and
_____ I'm pleased to say that I had passed all of
_____ them. I did particularly well in my maths
_____ exam, what I was really pleased about.
_____ Since then I've also started university.
_____ I told you, haven't I, that I'm studying
_____ economics at the university here in Bristol?
_____ I've made lots of new friends and the
_____ social life is great – though my parents
_____ keep telling me work harder. I'm still living
_____ at home, but I'd like to move into a flat
_____ with a couple of friends.
_____ I'm spending Christmas with my family,
_____ and then my friend Mike has invited me
_____ going skiing with him in France after New
_____ Year. That should be fun.
_____ Where you are spending Christmas?
_____ Do you go away?

_____ Have a great Christmas and New Year!

Emily

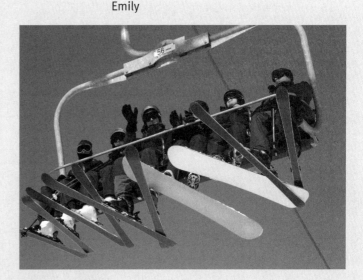

Mark /10

1 Complete the second sentence so that it means the same as the first. Include the word in brackets.

1 I wish you'd told me that you were going to be late. (might)

You _____ that you were going to be late.

2 You haven't eaten since breakfast. I'm sure you're hungry. (must)

You haven't eaten since breakfast. You

_____ .

3 It wasn't necessary to meet me at the airport. (needn't)

You _____ me at the airport.

4 I didn't phone you because I thought you were out. (would)

I _____ if I'd known you were in.

5 Don't walk alone in the park at night. (must)

You _____ alone in the park at night.

6 'I won't go to bed! It's only nine o'clock!' said Jamie. (refused)

Jamie _____ because it was only nine o'clock.

7 'Why didn't you phone me?' said John to Sally. (asked)

John _____ him.

8 How were you able to get across London in 45 minutes? (manage)

How _____ get across London in 45 minutes?

9 It's his arrogance that annoys me. (what)

_____ is his arrogance.

10 I don't particularly want to go out tonight. (feel like)

I _____ tonight.

Mark ___ /10

2 Complete the letter with the words in the box. You need to use some words more than once.

at	for	in	of	over	to	up	with

14th February

Dear Emily

I hope you had a good Christmas ¹_____ home with your family. I'm sorry I haven't written ²_____ a while, but I've been very busy ³_____ schoolwork. All ⁴_____ a sudden everybody is working really hard this term, and there's so much to learn. Of course, I'd be ⁵_____ a better position now if I'd worked a bit harder last year!

Did you receive my postcard from Florida last summer? You'll have realised when you read it that I didn't really take ⁶_____ camping! I hope your skiing holiday was more fun. I'd like to take ⁷_____ skiing – maybe you can teach me to ski if I come over to see you one day. It isn't that difficult, is it?

Next term, I'll be working even harder, so I might not have a great deal ⁸_____ time to write. But I promise to write more often as soon as my exams are ⁹_____.

That's all ¹⁰_____ now. Happy Valentine's Day!

Best wishes

Jack

Mark ___ /10

1 Complete the text with suitable words.

The first man in space

Yuri Gagarin was born in 1934 in a village, now renamed Gagarin, near Smolensk in Russia. His parents worked ¹_____ a farm, and his father was also a skilled carpenter. Yuri was ²_____ third of four children, and his elder sister helped to raise him while his parents worked. ³_____ a teenager he started work in a steelworks, at the ⁴_____ time continuing his studies at the technical high school in Saratov. While there, he joined the 'Aeroclub' and learned to fly ⁵_____ his spare time. He soon preferred flying to working in the steelworks, and on leaving college in 1955, he joined the air force and learned to fly fighter planes.

His daring and skill led to his being singled out for training in the Soviet space programme. Gagarin was only 1.57 metres tall. His small size was an advantage, as the spacecraft he ⁶_____ to fly in, *Vostok*, did not have ⁷_____ room inside for large people. *Vostok* was launched from the Baykonur site in the Kazakh desert on 12th April 1961. Although his flight around the Earth ⁸_____ only one hour and 45 minutes, Gagarin became the first person to travel into space and orbit the Earth.

After the flight, Gagarin became an instant celebrity, and ⁹_____ appearances all ¹⁰_____ the world to promote the Soviet achievement. He then returned to his former job, flying fighter planes. But on 27 March 1968, while on a training flight he died when he lost control of his plane and crashed. He was buried with honours alongside the wall of the Kremlin in Moscow's Red Square.

Mark /10

2 Find and correct ten more mistakes in this letter.

21st May

Dear Jack

_____ I've just moved into a new flat! At the

I'm sharing moment, (I share) it with two friends, but we

_____ might try to find a fourth person. It's great to

_____ be independent, although I miss sometimes

_____ my mum's cooking!

_____ Well, I'm halfway through the summer term

_____ and, to be honest, I haven't working hard

_____ enough. I'm quite worried for my exam

_____ results. (I've just been taking five exams!)

_____ How is your work going? You don't have

_____ exams at the end of the year, don't you?

_____ I think you should come to Britain when your

_____ term will have ended. There's lots to do here

_____ in Bristol in the summer, and you are able to

_____ stay at our flat. Our term finishes around the

_____ middle of June, so I won't work if you come

_____ in July.

_____ That's all for now. Sorry this letter is such

_____ short, but I'm exhausted. What I need that is

_____ a really long sleep!

Best wishes

Emily

Mark /10

FUNCTIONS BANK

ESTABLISHING THE TOPIC

The photos are connected with [the topic of] ... (1F)
... are to do with ... (1F)
... are linked by ... (1F)
... relate to ... (1F)
... show different aspects of ... (1F)

SPECULATING

It could be that ... or ... (1F)
It's hard to say whether ... or ... (1F)
Presumably, ... (1F)
I would guess that ... (1F)

DEDUCING

From their expressions, I'd say that ... (1F)
Judging by her expression, I'd say that ... (1F)
It's clear from their expressions that ... (1F)
They [look very happy], so clearly ... (1F)
They look as if they ... / as though they ... (1F)
It looks as if ... / as though ... (1F)
The fact that [they're smiling] would suggest that ... (1F)

PARAPHRASING

I don't know what it's called in English. (7F)
It's a kind of ... (7F)
It's like a ... (7F)
I mean ... (7F)
In other words, ... (7F)
... so to speak (7F)

TALKING ABOUT STATISTICS, GRAPHS AND CHARTS

A third / quarter of (people ...) (5F)
Two-thirds / three-fifths of (people ...) (5F)
One in three / ten (people ...) (5F)
Four out of five (people ...) (5F)
50% of (people ...) (5F)
increase / rise by 25% (5F)
decrease / fall by 10% (5F)
the number of ...
fell sharply / steadily (5F)
rose sharply / steadily (5F)
fluctuated (5F)
stayed the same (5F)
According to the chart/graph, ... (5F)
the majority of (people ...) (5F)
the percentage of (people who ...) (5F)

STRUCTURING YOUR PRESENTATION

I'd like to begin by saying ... (3F)
The first thing I'd like to say is that ... (3F)
First of all, ... / Firstly, ... (3F)
Secondly, ... (3F)
Finally, ... (3F)

OUTLINING THE ISSUE

Some people think that ... (10F)
Others maintain that ... (10F)

GIVING OPINIONS

I believe / I don't believe ... (3F)
In my view / opinion, ... (3F)
I agree with ... / I disagree with ... (3F)
As far as I'm concerned ... (10F)
Personally, I believe that ... (10F)
I'm convinced that ... (2D)
My view is that ... (10F)
The way I look at it, ... (10F)
My own view is that ... (10F)
To my mind, ... (1C)
One advantage / disadvantage of ... is that ... (2D)
There are strong arguments in favour of / against ... (2D)
I really think ...

EMPHASISING A POINT

We must remember that ... (6F)
There's no doubt in my mind that ... (6F)
Let's not forget that ... (6F)
I really do think that ... (6F)
It's important to bear in mind that ... (6F)
I believe very strongly that ... (6F)
I'm absolutely convinced that ... (6F)
Nobody could deny that ... (6F)
When it comes down to it, ... (8C)

GIVING EXAMPLES

For example, ... (3F)
For instance, ... (3F)
..., say, ... (3F)
I'm going to give some examples of ... (3F)
such as (10F)
To give you an example: ... (2D)

FUNCTIONS BANK

GIVING ADDITIONAL INFORMATION

What is more, … (3F)
Furthermore, … (3F)

ACKOWLEDGING AN OPPOSING POINT

It is true that … (10F)
I wouldn't deny that … (10F)
Of course, we have to accept that … (10F)
Admittedly, … (10F)

RE-STATING YOUR ORIGINAL POINT

However, this doesn't alter my view that … (10F)
But I would still say that … (10F)
But having said that, I still think that … (10F)
Nevertheless, I still believe that … (10F)

SUMMING UP

So, to sum up, … (3F)
In summary, then, … (3F)
It seems clear to me that … (3F)

AGREEING

I agree completely. (8F)
I couldn't agree more. (8F)
That's what I think too. (8F)
That's how I see it too. (8F)
I think you're absolutely right. (8F)
I think you're spot on. (8F)
I'd go along with that. (1C)
Absolutely. (1C)

PARTIALLY AGREEING

That's true, but … (7F)
I see your point but … (1C)
It may be true that … , but … (5D)
I admit that … . However, … (5D)
I'm willing to concede that … . Nevertheless, … (5D)

DISAGREEING

I totally disagree. (8F)
I'm afraid I disagree. (2D)
I really can't agree with you. (8F)
I take the opposite view. (8F)
I'm of the opposite opinion. (8F)
That's not how I see it at all. (8F)
That's not the way I look at it. (8F)
Surely you don't think that … (1C)
I'm not sure about that. (1C)
I think it's wrong to say that … (5D)
I disagree with the view that … (5D)
You have to admit that … (8C)

TALKING ABOUT PROS

The main benefit of … is … (2F)
… is generally a good thing because … (2F)
One positive aspect of … is (that) … (2F)

TALKING ABOUT CONS

On the other hand, … (2F)
As for the disadvantages, … (2F)
One disadvantage of … is (that) (2F)
Another drawback is (that) … (2F)
… is not a good idea because … (2F)

WRITING BANK

MAGAZINE ARTICLE

A Journey I Never Want to Repeat

Have you ever been in a situation where you thought you might die? That's what happened to me while I was on holiday in Greece two years ago.

We had been staying at a holiday resort on the mainland for nearly a week when we decided to visit one of the nearby islands. First, we booked the trip at our hotel, then we walked down to the harbour and found our boat. The captain welcomed us on board and we sat down near the front.

At first, the weather was good and the sea was calm. However, after about fifteen minutes, the wind became much stronger. Then dark clouds filled the sky, and it was clear that a storm was about to start. Ten minutes later, it was pouring with rain and the sea was extremely rough. It was absolutely terrifying!

The captain's voice came over the tannoy: 'We can't approach the island. I'm worried that we might hit the rocks if we go too close.' All we could do was wait for the storm to pass. Meanwhile, the boat was rocking violently from side to side and all of the passengers were feeling very ill as well as frightened. Finally, after about 45 minutes, when the storm passed and the sea became calm once more, we were able to finish our journey.

Being at sea during a storm isn't an experience I want to repeat. In future, I'll certainly check the weather forecasts before booking a boat trip!

- Think of a good title for the article (if one hasn't been specified in the exam task).
- Start your account with an introduction that will encourage your reader to continue reading. You can address the reader directly, especially with questions.
- Use an informal, lively style to maintain the reader's attention. You can use direct speech, exclamation marks and extreme adjectives.
- Divide your article into paragraphs.
- You can use sequencing expressions to order events or opinions.
- Finish your article with a definite conclusion, or a summary of what you have said. If appropriate give your opinion, or say how it affects your life now.

ESSAY (FOR AND AGAINST)

- Divide your essay into four paragraphs.
- Write an interesting introduction to your essay that will encourage your reader to continue reading.
- In the second paragraph include points in favour of the statement.
- In the third paragraph include points against the statement.
- The fourth paragraph should be a conclusion balancing the arguments for and against the statement and offering your own opinion.
- Use linking expressions such as *As a result*, *On the other hand*, *Furthermore*, *On balance* to guide your reader through your essay.

'Students shouldn't have to pay to study at university.' Discuss.

Although the government gives money to universities, students still have to pay for their university education. They pay tuition fees and also need money to live on while they are studying. However, some people argue that education should be free, including university education.

It is hard to deny that poorer people in our society sometimes miss the chance to study at university because they cannot afford it. As a result, they have fewer opportunities when they apply for jobs, and often remain at a disadvantage throughout their lives. This is unfair. Free university education would ensure that everybody has an equal chance to study at a higher level. In addition, it would mean that universities could attract the most able students and not the wealthiest.

On the other hand, free university education would cost the government a lot of money and they would have to raise this money through taxation. Some people maintain that it is unfair to tax ordinary working people so that a minority can study at university. Furthermore, they question how useful university education really is for the country as a whole, and argue that vocational training would be more beneficial.

On balance, I believe that the advantages of providing free university education outweigh the disadvantages. While free education costs everybody a little more in taxes, it creates a fairer system and more opportunities for poorer people to do well.

WRITING BANK

ESSAY (OPINION)

'Large, powerful cars are a danger to everyone and should be banned.' Do you agree? Why? Why not?

Few people would deny that global warming is a serious problem, and that reducing carbon emissions is the main way to tackle it. Large, powerful cars produce far more carbon emissions than cars with small engines, and for this reason,
I believe they should be banned.

First and foremost, large cars with very powerful engines are completely unnecessary in today's world. Our city streets are full of these vehicles, crawling along at ten kilometres per hour and creating huge amounts of pollution. An electric car would be just as fast in a busy city and would produce no carbon emissions at all.

Moreover, large cars are more dangerous for pedestrians and cyclists because they are heavier and more likely to cause serious injury or death if there is a collision. At a time when we are encouraging people to walk or cycle instead of driving, we should aim to make our streets as safe as possible, and that includes banning unnecessarily large cars.

Of course, not everybody would agree with this position. Some people maintain that they have a genuine need for a very large car. For example, families with a lot of children may claim that only large vehicles, or 'people carriers' as they are sometimes known, provide enough room.

All things considered, I really do think that large, powerful cars should be made illegal. While it's true that they are useful for some families, they create an unacceptable amount of pollution and cause irreversible damage to the environment.

- Divide your essay into five paragraphs.
- Write an interesting introduction to your essay that will encourage your reader to continue reading. Include your own opinion.
- In the second paragraph, include the main point in support of your opinion.
- In the third paragraph, include another point in support of your opinion.
- In the fourth paragraph, include points in support of the opposite opinion.
- The fifth paragraph should be a conclusion. Restate your opinion, but briefly mention the opposite side of the argument as well.
- Use linking expressions such as *First and foremost*, *Moreover*, *For example*, *All things considered* to guide your reader through your essay.

DESCRIPTION OF A PERSON

- In the first paragraph, include the name of the person, what he or she does, and the reason for your choice.
- The second paragraph should include a physical description.
- In the third paragraph, mention the person's main characteristics and give examples.
- The fourth paragraph should explain what makes this person special, with examples of behaviour and achievements.
- The final paragraph should sum up your thoughts about the person.

It is sometimes difficult to think of famous people who are good role models. However, I have always admired the actress Rachel Weisz because she is not only beautiful but also intelligent and principled.

Rachel Weisz is 170 centimetres tall and has long, dark hair and brown eyes. Although she was born in England, her father was born in Hungary and her mother in Austria. Her mixed cultural background no doubt contributes to her exotic beauty.

Undeniably, Weisz has always been one of the most thoughtful and intelligent stars of the big screen. For example, aged fourteen, she turned down work as a model and actress because she was worried that it would interfere with her education. She completed an English degree at Cambridge University before launching her career in films.

Because of her beauty, Weisz is offered roles in all kinds of romantic blockbusters, but she is very careful about which parts she accepts. One of her most successful roles was in the Oscar-winning 2005 film, 'The Constant Gardener', which is about corruption in Kenya. It is a mark of her caring attitude that, during the film, she and her co-stars set up a charity called the Constant Gardener Trust to help people in Kenya who are living in poverty.

In my opinion, Rachel Weisz is a good role model because she has never allowed fame to go to her head. Although she is very successful, she still spends time helping people who are less fortunate than herself.

WRITING BANK

DESCRIPTION OF A PLACE

Of all the cities I have visited, the one I like most is Barcelona. I spent five days there in 2007 when I was on holiday with my parents and it made a big impression on me.

Barcelona is a large city in the north-east of Spain, in a region called Catalonia. It is situated on the Mediterranean coast about 150 kilometres south of the Pyrenees. The city itself is quite hilly, and there are mountains to the north-west, including the famous Montserrat where there is a Benedictine abbey which can be reached by cable car.

There are many beautiful places to visit within the city. There are parks and beaches, as well as a busy port which was renovated in preparation for the Olympic Games in 1992. In the heart of the city, you can find Las Ramblas, which are wide streets full of pedestrians, cafés and street performers.

My favourite building in Barcelona is the huge church called the Sagrada Familia, which was designed by the Catalan architect Antoni Gaudí. Although work began on the church in 1882, it has never been completed and continues to this day. However, it is open to visitors, who can climb the incredibly tall towers and enjoy amazing views across the city.

Barcelona is a great place to visit because it has so many different things to offer: beaches, parks, architecture and culture. It also has a modern and lively atmosphere which I love.

- In the first paragraph, include the name of the place and the reason for your choice.
- The second paragraph should describe the general location and landscape of the place.
- In the third paragraph, describe what the place has to offer: notable landmarks, facilities, etc.
- In the fourth paragraph, give a more detailed description of one particular aspect or part of the place.
- The final paragraph should sum up your thoughts about the place.

FILM REVIEW

- Include information about the title and genre of the film, its director and the main actor or actors in the first paragraph.
- Outline the plot in the second paragraph.
- Say what you liked and did not like about it in the third paragraph.
- In the final paragraph, say who you would recommend the film to and why.

One of the best films that I have seen recently is called 'The Bourne Ultimatum', an action movie directed by Paul Greengrass and starring Matt Damon. It is based on a novel by Robert Ludlum and is the third and final part of a trilogy about the same character, Jason Bourne; the first is called 'The Bourne Identity', and the second is 'The Bourne Supremacy'.

The film tells the story of Jason Bourne, a trained assassin who remembers nothing about his past life or the organisation that trained him. All he knows is that a new generation of assassins is now trying to kill him. He needs to find the people behind this organisation and put a stop to their activities, before they put a stop to him!

The pace of the film is frantic and the action is non-stop. In general, the acting is excellent and Matt Damon in particular gives a great performance. The only flaw in the film is that there are a few places where the plot is not very realistic. For example, at one point, Jason Bourne is involved in a horrific car crash but walks away completely uninjured.

In my opinion, 'The Bourne Ultimatum' is the best of the three films in the trilogy. The minor problems with the plot are outweighed by the fact that the film has you on the edge of your seat from start to finish. I would certainly recommend it to anybody looking for a thrilling and fast-paced action film.

WRITING BANK

BOOK REVIEW

One of the best books that I have read in the past year is called 'Holes'. It's by an American writer called Louis Sachar and is his best known novel.

'Holes' tells the story of a boy called Stanley Yelnats, who is wrongly convicted of a crime and sent to an institution for young offenders in the middle of the Texan desert called Camp Green Lake. There he and the other offenders spend their days digging holes in the sand as punishment. The camp's motto is: 'If you take a bad boy and make him dig a hole every day in the hot sun, it will turn him into a good boy'. The plot really comes alive when Stanley and his friend, Zero, decide to escape from the camp and set off across the desert.

The main strengths of the book are its exciting plot and well-developed characterisation. None of the inmates at Camp Green Lake is a stereotype; they are all believable characters. The novel is quite complex, mixing the story of Stanley with two other stories set in the past. At the end of the book, these stories come together in a series of coincidences. It's a clever ending, but perhaps a little too neat to be totally convincing.

Although this entertaining and thought-provoking novel is aimed at teenagers, I would recommend it for adults too. It is certainly a book I will remember for a long time.

- Include information about the title of the book and the author in the first paragraph.
- Outline the plot in the second paragraph.
- Say what you liked and did not like about it in the third paragraph.
- In the final paragraph, say who you would recommend the book to and why.

FORMAL LETTER

- Start *Dear Sir or Madam* if you don't know the name of the person you are writing to. Use the person's title (Mr, Mrs, Ms) and their surname if you do (Dear Mrs Samson).
- State your reason for writing in the first paragraph.
- Avoid contractions.
- Use formal expressions.
- Use a phrase to bring your letter to a close.
- End your letter with *Yours faithfully* if you started with *Dear Sir or Madam*, and *Yours sincerely* if you started with the person's title and surname.
- Sign your name and print it in full afterwards.
- Use the abbreviation *enc.* if you are including anything with the letter such as a CV, an application form, a reference.

Dear Sir or Madam,

I am writing to apply for the temporary post of Summer Camp Activity Co-ordinator, as advertised in The Times last Saturday.

I am a second year student at Bristol University and am currently taking my end-of-year exams. The summer vacation begins on 21st June and ends on 23rd September, and I am hoping to find a job for as much of that period as possible.

Last summer, I worked for a company called Sunny Days which organises holidays for children with disabilities. My duties included arranging sports and other activities and taking the children for excursions. I was considered to be a hard-working and responsible employee, and my manager at Sunny Days has already offered to provide a reference, should you require one.

I am enclosing my Curriculum Vitae and I look forward to hearing from you in due course.

Yours faithfully,

Kevin Waterstone

Kevin Waterstone
enc. CV

GRAMMAR REFERENCE

Unit 1

Present perfect simple

We use the present perfect for actions that happened at an unspecified time in the past. We also use the present perfect for actions that have recently been completed.

I've visited Paris so many times.

Dave's had a motorbike accident. He's in hospital at the moment.

Present perfect continuous

We use the present perfect continuous for actions that started in the past and are still in progress.

Hermione's been going out with Frank for six months. They're very happy.

Past simple

We use the past simple for an action that happened at a specific time in the past and to describe a sequence of short actions in the past.

My grandfather got married in 1945.

I went to the shops, bought a book and then went to a café.

The past continuous

We use the past continuous to describe longer actions in the past. It is often used in conjunction with the past simple, which describes a short action that interrupts a longer one.

It was raining.

Children were playing in the park.

Jack was reading his newspaper when he heard a scream.

Past perfect simple

We use the past perfect simple to talk about a completed event or action that happened before another event or action at a specific time in the past.

Penny had heard all about the man in the grey suit before she met him at Joe's Café.

Past perfect continuous

We use the past perfect continuous with action verbs and *for* and *since* to say how long an action had been in progress before a specific time in the past. We also use it to show the cause of something that happened in the past. We don't use the past perfect continuous with state verbs such as *be*, *know*, *like*, etc.

Simon had been driving for two hours when he realised someone was following him.

Sir Malcolm was exhausted. He'd been playing golf all afternoon.

Unit 2

Determiners

Determiners are used before a noun and include articles (*a*, *an* and *the*) and quantifiers (*all*, *any*, *both*, *each*, *every*, *few*, etc.). Most quantifiers can be used with the preposition *of*, e.g. *most of*, *a few of*, *several of*.

Most of the people in the room had known about the surprise guest.

However, *no* and *every* cannot be used in this way. Instead, *none of* and *every one of* are used.

None of the hotels were suitable for such important visitors.

Verb patterns

Some verbs are only followed by the -*ing* form (*avoid*, *enjoy*, *imagine*, *feel*, *suggest*, *consider*, etc.) and some verbs are only followed by the infinitive form (*agree*, *decide*, *expect*, *happen*, *manage*, *want*, etc.).

Some of the possible verb + infinitive structures are:

verb + infinitive (*agree*, *promise*, *seem*, *expect*, *refuse*, *want*, etc.)

Mark has agreed to work with Richard on the new project.

verb + object + infinitive with *to* (*force*, *persuade*, *allow*, *inspire*, etc.)

My mum allowed me to drive her car to the beach.

verb + object + past participle (*get* and *have*)

Rebecca had her hair cut in the new hairdresser's on Cowley Road.

There are also some verbs that can be followed by both an -*ing* form and an infinitive form but with a difference in meaning (*remember*, *try*, *go on*, *stop*, etc.).

I remember meeting Lord Lucan in Mozambique in 1975.

Did you remember to lock the door this morning?

GRAMMAR REFERENCE

Unit 3

will

We use *will* to talk about future facts and predictions. It is also used to make instant decisions about the present and to make offers and promises.

I will be 21 in June. I'm so excited.

I'll buy you a new coat for your birthday.

going to

We use *going to* to talk about future plans that we have already made. It is also used to make predictions about the future based on what is happening now.

Tony's going to take us to Great Yarmouth on Sunday. Do you want to come?

Look at that man in the red shirt. I think he's going to come over here.

Present continuous

The present continuous is used for future arrangements. It is often used to talk about future plans that we have made with other people.

I'm meeting Alicia for drinks tonight and Harry and Chelsea are coming round for dinner tomorrow.

Present simple

The present simple is used to talk about future events that are scheduled or timetabled.

The bus leaves at 2.15 p.m. and the match starts at 3 p.m.

Future continuous

The future continuous is used to talk about an action that will be in progress in the future. It is also used to talk about something that we expect will happen, and to make polite enquiries.

This time next year we'll be living in Hawaii.

She'll probably be cooking dinner when I get home.

Will you be wanting ice with your martini, Mr Bond?

Future perfect

The future perfect is used to talk about a completed action or event in the future. The future perfect continuous is used to say how long an action in the future has been in progress for.

By 2012 we'll have been married for 25 years.

Alex will have been driving for eight hours by the time he arrives here.

Unit 4

Talking about ability

We usually use *can* or *can't* to talk about ability in the present.

Phoebe can speak three languages.

We normally use *will be able to* to talk about ability in the future, although we can use *can* and *can't* when we want to talk about future arrangements.

The baby will be able to talk in a year's time.

I can meet you on Friday but I can't see you at the weekend.

We only use *could* to talk about general ability in the past. We also use *could* with verbs of perception such as *see, hear, taste, feel* and *smell*.

I could swim 100 metres when I was ten years old.

When we talk about past ability on one occasion we use expressions like *managed to do* or *succeeded in doing*. However, we can use *could* with verbs of perception to talk about one occasion in the past, and we can also use the negative form, *couldn't*, to talk about ability in the past on one occasion.

In 1996 Arthur managed to climb Mount Everest. On the peak he could see an amazing view of the Himalayas. He couldn't take any photos, though, because his hands were too cold.

Nominal clauses

Nominal clauses function as nouns in a sentence. They often begin with *that*. In formal sentences it is possible to begin a sentence with a nominal clause that begins with *that*. In informal English, it is usual to use *it* followed by *is, seems, appears*, etc.

That he spoke to you first is unusual.

It's unusual that he spoke to you first.

Nominal clauses can also begin with *what* and *all*. What is used to mean 'the thing which' and *all* is used to mean 'everything which'.

What I like best about this job are the working hours.

All we have achieved in this world we must be thankful for.

Unit 5

Reported speech

Tenses, personal and possessive pronouns, time expressions and demonstrative adjectives are all often changed when we use reported speech.

'I'm going to meet you tomorrow night,' said Chris.
Chris said he was going to meet her the following evening.

When the reporting verb is in the present simple or the present perfect we don't normally change the tense of the verb in the reported sentence. Neither do we change the tense if we are reporting a past perfect verb or *would, could, should* and *had better*.

'I'm the best player in the world.'
Ronaldo says he's the best player in the world.

'You could do a lot better than this,' said the teacher.
The teacher said we could do a lot better than that.

In reported questions we make the same tense changes as in reported statements. The word order changes in reported questions and we add *if / whether* when we report questions that require *yes / no* answers.

'Where's your mother?' asked the police officer.
The police officer asked where my mother was.

'Would you like a cup of coffee?' asked the waiter.
The waiter asked me if I would like a cup of coffee.

Reporting verbs

Apart from *say* and *tell* there are a number of verbs that can be used to introduce reported statements. These verbs are used with a variety of structures.

verb + infinitive with *to*

We offered to help.

verb + object + infinitive with *to*

I reminded him to do his homework.

verb + gerund

Sam suggested going for a pizza.

verb + preposition + gerund

He's always boasting of being a good footballer.

verb + object + preposition + gerund

She warned us against smoking.

verb + *that* + *should*-clause

He requested that we should pay for it.

Unit 6

Question forms

Question words such as *what, where, who,* etc. are used to make subject and object questions.

In object questions the question words are the objects of the question. We use auxiliary verbs between the question word and the subject of the question.

Where did Maria go? She went to the shop to buy some milk.

In subject questions the question words are the subjects of the questions. We don't use auxiliary verbs in these questions:

Who lives in the old house? Jeff Delaware lives there. He's 95.

In indirect questions we use affirmative word order and verb forms after the question words.

I'd like to know where Maria went yesterday.

Question tags

Question tags are used to turn statements into questions. We add negative tags to affirmative statements, and affirmative tags to negative statements. If the statement includes an auxiliary or modal verb, this is repeated in the tag. If there isn't an auxiliary verb or a modal verb in the statement, we use *do* or *did*.

You're Professor Simpson's wife, aren't you?
Brian doesn't like coffee, does he?

Tag questions

Tag questions are used to respond to a statement. Affirmative tag questions are used with affirmative statements and negative tag questions are used with negative statements.

Octopuses are very intelligent.   Are they?
Sarah doesn't like flying.   Doesn't she?

Unit 7

Advice, obligation and prohibition

We often use *must* when the speaker wants to express their own feelings about the importance or necessity of something. When the obligation is external and comes from other people, we often prefer to use *have to*.

I really must phone my parents tonight.

You have to pay income tax when you get a job.

We use *should* and *ought to* to express advice.

You should see a doctor about that cough.

You ought to take more exercise.

GRAMMAR REFERENCE

We use *must* to express obligation or an order.

Hard hats must be worn on the building site.

We use *mustn't* to express prohibition.

Visitors mustn't feed the animals.

We use *have to* to express obligation.

Passengers have to wear seat belts.

We use *need* to express necessity.

We need to buy some food before we go into the jungle.

We use *don't have to* and *needn't* to express lack of necessity.

Cyclists don't have to wear crash helmets in Britain.

Speculating

Modal verbs are used to talk about the certainty or the possibility of something happening.

In the present we use *must* and *can't* to talk about certainty.

It must be John. Who else would call on us at this time?

It can't be Mary. She's in New York all week.

We use *might*, *may* and *could* to talk about possibility.

It might be Kathmandu but it could be Lhasa.

In the past we use *must have* and *can't have* to talk about certainty. We use *might have*, *may have* and *could have* to talk about possibility.

A bird can't have eaten the meat. It might have been a fox or a dog.

Unit 8

Modals in the past

We use *should have* and *ought to have* + past participle to say what the right thing to do was.

Mary really should have told Barnaby that she was going out with Peter.

We use *might have* and *could have* + past participle to complain that somebody didn't do the right thing.

You could have done the washing up before you left the house.

We use *needn't have* + past participle to talk about something which happened but wasn't necessary.

I needn't have brought a sleeping bag as there were plenty of blankets.

We use *didn't need to* + infinitive to talk about something which didn't happen because it wasn't necessary.

I didn't need to go shopping this morning because Joanna had ordered everything online.

Mixed conditionals

We use the third conditional to refer to hypothetical situations in the past and the second conditional to refer hypothetical situations in the present or future.

If I had been older, I would have asked her to marry me.

If he were a millionaire, he'd build a new hospital for the poor.

A mixed conditional refers to both the past and the present. It combines both the third conditional and the second conditional.

If we hadn't gone the wrong way, we would be at the party now.

If I were American, I would have voted for a different president.

Unit 9

Habitual behaviour in the present

We use the present simple, often with an adverb of frequency, to talk about habits and routines in the present. However, when we want to comment on someone's annoying habits in the present we use the present continuous with *always*. We can also suggest irritation by stressing *will* when we comment on someone's habits.

Matthew gets up every day at half past seven.

He's always slamming the door when he leaves the house.

He <u>will</u> speak when we're trying to watch TV.

Habitual behaviour in the past

We use *used to* to talk about past states and habits. We also use *would* to talk about past habits, but not states. We can also suggest irritation by stressing *would* when we comment on someone's habits.

My granddad used to ride a motorbike to work.

When they were children, they would go swimming every summer.

She <u>would</u> always keep everyone waiting.

Future in the past

We use *was going to* + infinitive without *to* when we talk about past things which were still in the future at that time. We also use *was about to* in this way.

Ashley was going to leave the house when he noticed the kitchen was on fire.

Belinda was about to panic when she remembered what her mother had said.

Was to and was to have

We use *was to* + infinitive without *to* to talk about the future in the past. We use it when we talk about something that actually happened.

Grandpa Joe was to live in that house for the rest of his life.

We use *was to have* + past participle to talk about something we expected to happen but didn't.

I was to have started a new job in Cairo when I heard the terrible news.

Unit 10

Passive

The passive is formed with the correct form of the verb *be* + past participle. The passive is used when we don't want to say, or we can't say, who performed the action.

Oh no! My house has been burgled!
The train has been delayed by 32 minutes.

The passive is also used to put the main focus at the beginning of the sentence. If we want to say who carried out the action we introduce the person's name with the preposition *by*.

The president has been shot dead while on holiday.
Liverpool were beaten by Horsham in the FA Cup last night.

Passives with verbs such as *know* and *believe*

Verbs such as *know, believe, think,* etc. are often used in the passive form after the subject *it*.

it + passive (present or past) + *that*

It is believed by some people that aliens exist.

These verbs are also frequently used in the following passive structure.

subject + passive (present or past) + *to do / to have done*

The sun was thought to go around the earth.
Aliens are thought to have started the human race.

Passive verbs with two objects

Verbs such as *give, offer, send, award, show,* etc. often have two objects, a person and a thing. Either of these objects can become the subject of a passive structure. The choice depends on what you want to make the main focus of the sentence.

Bobby Davro was awarded the Oscar for Best Supporting Actor.

WORDLIST

Word	Phonetics	Translation	Word	Phonetics	Translation

Unit 1 Against the odds

Word	Phonetics	Translation
argumentative (a)	/ˌɑːgjuˈmentətɪv/	....
big-headed (a)	/ˌbɪgˈhedɪd/	....
bow (v)	/baʊ/	....
broad-minded (a)	/ˌbrɔːdˈmaɪndɪd/	....
cheerful (a)	/ˈtʃɪəfl/	....
clamber (v)	/ˈklæmbə(r)/	....
compliant (a)	/kəmˈplaɪənt/	....
considerate (a)	/kənˈsɪdərət/	....
costume (n)	/ˈkɒstjuːm/	....
courteous (a)	/ˈkɜːtiəs/	....
dependable (a)	/dɪˈpendəbl/	....
deteriorate (v)	/dɪˈtɪəriəreɪt/	....
determined (a)	/dɪˈtɜːmɪnd/	....
devotion (n)	/dɪˈvəʊʃn/	....
drift (v)	/drɪft/	....
earnest (a)	/ˈɜːnɪst/	....
filthy (a)	/ˈfɪlθi/	....
flag (v)	/flæg/	....
flexible (a)	/ˈfleksəbl/	....
furious (a)	/ˈfjʊəriəs/	....
generous (a)	/ˈdʒenərəs/	....
grab (v)	/græb/	....
grumpy (a)	/ˈgrʌmpi/	....
haul (v)	/hɔːl/	....
hideous (a)	/ˈhɪdiəs/	....
horrified (a)	/ˈhɒrɪfaɪd/	....
hot-headed (a)	/ˌhɒtˈhedɪd/	....
ill-mannered (a)	/ˌɪlˈmænəd/	....
inconsiderate (a)	/ˌɪnkənˈsɪdərət/	....
inflate (v)	/ɪnˈfleɪt/	....
inhibited (a)	/ɪnˈhɪbɪtɪd/	....
insecure (a)	/ˌɪnsɪˈkjʊə(r)/	....
jovial (a)	/ˈdʒəʊviəl/	....
level-headed (a)	/ˌlevlˈhedɪd/	....
line (of a play) (n)	/laɪn/	....
methodical (a)	/məˈθɒdɪkl/	....
miserable (a)	/ˈmɪzrəbl/	....
modest (a)	/ˈmɒdɪst/	....
naïve (a)	/naɪˈiːv/	....
narrow-minded (a)	/ˌnærəʊˈmaɪndɪd/	....
obstinate (a)	/ˈɒbstɪnət/	....
outgoing (a)	/ˌaʊtˈgəʊɪŋ/	....
pour (v)	/pɔː(r)/	....
presumably (adv)	/prɪˈzuːməbli/	....
pretentious (a)	/prɪˈtenʃəs/	....
prompter (n)	/ˈprɒmptə(r)/	....
relieved (a)	/rɪˈliːvd/	....
reserved (a)	/rɪˈzɜːvd/	....
resigned (a)	/rɪˈzaɪnd/	....
rot (v)	/rɒt/	....
self-confident (a)	/ˌselfˈkɒnfɪdənt/	....
shake (v)	/ʃeɪk/	....
slump (v)	/slʌmp/	....
sob (v)	/sɒb/	....
sophisticated (a)	/səˈfɪstɪkeɪtɪd/	....
spontaneous (a)	/spɒnˈteɪniəs/	....
stubborn (a)	/ˈstʌbən/	....
superficial (a)	/ˌsuːpəˈfɪʃl/	....
thoughtful (a)	/ˈθɔːtfl/	....
thoughtless (a)	/ˈθɔːtləs/	....
tight-fisted (a)	/ˌtaɪtˈfɪstɪd/	....
tolerant (a)	/ˈtɒlərənt/	....
unassuming (a)	/ˌʌnəˈsjuːmɪŋ/	....
unreliable (a)	/ˌʌnrɪˈlaɪəbl/	....
unsystematic (a)	/ˌʌnsɪstəˈmætɪk/	....
voracious (a)	/vəˈreɪʃəs/	....

Get ready for your exam 1

Word	Phonetics	Translation
administer (v)	/ədˈmɪnɪstə(r)/	....
dispense (v)	/dɪˈspens/	....
epidemic (n)	/ˌepɪˈdemɪk/	....
harness (n)	/ˈhɑːnəs/	....
lead (n)	/liːd/	....
legendary (a)	/ˈledʒəndri/	....
subsidise (v)	/ˈsʌbsɪdaɪz/	....
tend (v)	/tend/	....
unabashed (a)	/ˌʌnəˈbæʃt/	....

Unit 2 For what it's worth

Word	Phonetics	Translation
(un)furnished (a)	/ˈfɜːnɪʃt/	....
amenities (n)	/əˈmiːnətiz/	....
bargain (n)	/ˈbɑːgən/	....
barn (n)	/bɑːn/	....
basement (n)	/ˈbeɪsmənt/	....
block (n)	/blɒk/	....
bolt (v)	/bɒlt/	....
character (n)	/ˈkærəktə(r)/	....
conversion (n)	/kənˈvɜːʃn/	....
credit (n)	/ˈkredɪt/	....
dear (a)	/dɪə(r)/	....
debt (n)	/det/	....
detached (a)	/dɪˈtætʃt/	....
enterprising (a)	/ˈentəpraɪzɪŋ/	....
exploitation (n)	/ˌeksplɔɪˈteɪʃn/	....
financial (a)	/faɪˈnænʃl/	....
fortune (n)	/ˈfɔːtjuːn/	....
gas central heating (n)	/ˌgæs sentrəl ˈhiːtɪŋ/	....
genuine (a)	/ˈdʒenjuɪn/	....
greed (n)	/griːd/	....
hard up (a)	/ˌhɑːd ˈʌp/	....
lease (n)	/liːs/	....
linen (n)	/ˈlɪnɪn/	....
mains (n)	/meɪnz/	....
open-plan (a)	/ˌəʊpənˈplæn/	....
ostensibly (adv)	/ɒˈstensəbli/	....
overpriced (a)	/ˌəʊvəˈpraɪst/	....
period (a)	/ˈpɪəriəd/	....
precariousness (n)	/prɪˈkeəriəsnəs/	....
precious (a)	/ˈpreʃəs/	....
priceless (a)	/ˈpraɪsləs/	....
profit (n)	/ˈprɒfɪt/	....
prosaically (adv)	/prəˈzeɪɪkli/	....
rent (n)	/rent/	....
rip off (phr v)	/ˌrɪp ˈɒf/	....
rye (n)	/raɪ/	....
slink (v)	/slɪŋk/	....
splash out (phr v)	/ˌsplæʃ ˈaʊt/	....
stampede (n)	/stæmˈpiːd/	....
status (n)	/ˈsteɪtəs/	....
stroke (n)	/strəʊk/	....
tenant (n)	/ˈtenənt/	....
warehouse (n)	/ˈweəhaʊs/	....
well-off (a)	/ˌwelˈɒf/	....
worthless (a)	/ˈwɜːθləs/	....

Get ready for your exam 2

Word	Phonetics	Translation
benefactor (n)	/ˈbenɪfæktə(r)/	....
enamel (n)	/ɪˈnæml/	....
staggered (a)	/ˈstægəd/	....

WORDLIST

Word	Phonetics	Translation

Unit 3 From cradle to grave

Word	Phonetics	Translation
adolescence (n)	/ˌædəˈlesəns/	....
adulthood (n)	/ˈædʌlthʊd/	....
answer back (phr v)	/ˌɑːnsə ˈbæk/	....
bald (a)	/bɔːld/	....
ban (v)	/bæn/	....
bash (v)	/bæʃ/	....
be born (v)	/bi ˈbɔːn/	....
be brought up (v)	/bi ˌbrɔːt ˈʌp/	....
be buried (v)	/bi ˈberid/	....
bob (n)	/bɒb/	....
bossy (a)	/ˈbɒsi/	....
bring out (phr v)	/ˌbrɪŋ ˈaʊt/	....
brush under the carpet (idiom)	/ˌbrʌʃ ʌndə ðə ˈkɑːpɪt/	....
care home (n)	/ˈkeə həʊm/	....
childhood (n)	/ˈtʃaɪldhʊd/	....
combative (a)	/ˈkɒmbətɪv/	....
come down to (phr v)	/kʌm ˈdaʊn tə/	....
confusing (a)	/kənˈfjuːzɪŋ/	....
conscientious (a)	/ˌkɒnʃiˈenʃəs/	....
cotton wool (n)	/ˌkɒtn ˈwʊl/	....
crew cut (n)	/ˈkruːkʌt/	....
cut down (on sth) (phr v)	/ˌkʌt ˈdaʊn ɒn/	....
decisive (a)	/dɪˈsaɪsɪv/	....
diligent (a)	/ˈdɪlɪdʒənt/	....
disruptive (a)	/dɪsˈrʌptɪv/	....
do sth up (phr v)	/ˌduː ˈʌp/	....
dump (v)	/dʌmp/	....
end up (phr v)	/ˌend ˈʌp/	....
engagement (n)	/ɪnˈɡeɪdʒmənt/	....
frank (a)	/fræŋk/	....
freckles (n)	/ˈfreklz/	....
gain (v)	/ɡeɪn/	....
get on with (phr v)	/ˌɡet ˈɒn wɪð/	....
get sb down (phr v)	/ˌɡet ˈdaʊn/	....
graveyard (n)	/ˈɡreɪvjɑːd/	....
grow up (phr v)	/ˌɡrəʊ ˈʌp/	....
growl (v)	/ɡraʊl/	....
grown-up (n)	/ˈɡrəʊnʌp/	....
hold sth/sb up (phr v)	/ˌhəʊld ˈʌp/	....
inadvertently (adv)	/ˌɪnədˈvɜːtəntli/	....
infancy (n)	/ˈɪnfənsi/	....
isolated (a)	/ˈaɪsəleɪtɪd/	....
jet off (phr v)	/ˌdʒet ˈɒf/	....
kid (n)	/kɪd/	....
look down on sb (phr v)	/ˌlʊk ˈdaʊn ɒn/	....
marginalise (v)	/ˈmɑːdʒɪnəlaɪz/	....
maturely (adv)	/məˈtʃʊəli/	....
middle age (n)	/ˌmɪdl ˈeɪdʒ/	....
moan (v)	/məʊn/	....
moody (a)	/ˈmuːdi/	....
moustache (n)	/məˈstɑːʃ/	....
OAP (n)	/ˌəʊ eɪ ˈpiː/	....
old age (n)	/ˌəʊld ˈeɪdʒ/	....
own up (to sth)(phr v)	/ˌəʊn ˈʌp/	....
pale-skinned (a)	/ˌpeɪlˈskɪnd/	....
pass away (phr v)	/ˌpɑːs əˈweɪ/	....
past it (a)	/ˈpɑːst ɪt/	....
pension (n)	/ˈpenʃn/	....
plump (a)	/plʌmp/	....
ponytails (n)	/ˈpəʊniteɪlz/	....
put sb down (phr v)	/ˌpʊt ˈdaʊn/	....
put sth down to (phr v)	/ˌpʊt ˈdaʊn tə/	....
put up with sth/sb (phr v)	/ˌpʊt ˈʌp wɪð/	....
quick-tempered (a)	/ˌkwɪkˈtempəd/	....
reasonable (a)	/ˈriːznəbl/	....
rebel (v)	/rɪˈbel/	....
receding hairline (n)	/rɪˌsiːdɪŋ ˈheəlaɪn/	....

Word	Phonetics	Translation
retire (v)	/rɪˈtaɪə(r)/	....
rosy-cheeked (a)	/ˌrəʊziˈtʃiːkt/	....
round-faced (a)	/ˌraʊndˈfeɪst/	....
row (v)	/raʊ/	....
scruffy (a)	/ˈskrʌfi/	....
set sth up (phr v)	/ˌset ˈʌp/	....
settle down (phr v)	/ˌsetl ˈdaʊn/	....
shabby (a)	/ˈʃæbi/	....
shrewd (a)	/ʃruːd/	....
storm out (phr v)	/ˌstɔːm ˈaʊt/	....
stuck in a rut (idiom)	/ˌstʌk ɪn ə ˈrʌt/	....
toddler (n)	/ˈtɒdlə(r)/	....
turn into (phr v)	/ˌtɜːn ˈɪntə/	....
unpredictable (a)	/ˌʌnprɪˈdɪktəbl/	....
well-dressed (a)	/ˌwelˈdrest/	....
witty (a)	/ˈwɪti/	....
wrinkles (n)	/ˈrɪŋklz/	....
youth (n)	/juːθ/	....

Get ready for your exam 3

Word	Phonetics	Translation
ancestry (n)	/ˈænsestri/	....
chronicle (v)	/ˈkrɒnɪkl/	....
diagnose (v)	/ˈdaɪəɡnəʊz/	....
painstakingly (adv)	/ˈpeɪnsteɪkɪŋli/	....
resolve (v)	/rɪˈzɒlv/	....
start the ball rolling (idiom)	/ˌstɑːt ðə ˈbɔːl ˌrəʊlɪŋ/	....
stumble upon sth/sb (phr v)	/ˈstʌmbl əˌpɒn/	....
swap (v)	/swɒp/	....
tap dance (n)	/ˈtæp dɑːns/	....
track down (phr v)	/ˌtræk ˈdaʊn/	....
unearth (v)	/ʌnˈɜːθ/	....

Unit 4 Man and beast

Word	Phonetics	Translation
animal rights (n)	/ˌænɪml ˈraɪts/	....
antennae (n)	/ænˈteniː/	....
antlers (n)	/ˈæntləz/	....
bark (v)	/bɑːk/	....
beak (n)	/biːk/	....
boar (n)	/bɔː(r)/	....
bull (n)	/bʊl/	....
bunch (n)	/bʌntʃ/	....
buzz (v)	/bʌz/	....
calf (n)	/kɑːf/	....
cattle(n)	/ˈkætl/	....
chatter (v)	/ˈtʃætə(r)/	....
chick (n)	/tʃɪk/	....
claw (n)	/klɔː/	....
cockerel (n)	/ˈkɒkərəl/	....
colony (n)	/ˈkɒləni/	....
console (n)	/ˈkɒnsəʊl/	....
damage (n)	/ˈdæmɪdʒ/	....
dense (a)	/dens/	....
dog collar (n)	/ˈdɒɡ ˌkɒlə(r)/	....
evolve (v)	/ɪˈvɒlv/	....
ewe (n)	/juː/	....
exceptionally (adv)	/ɪkˈsepʃənəli/	....
fang (n)	/fæŋ/	....
feather (n)	/ˈfeðə(r)/	....
fin (n)	/fɪn/	....
flock (n)	/flɒk/	....
foal (n)	/fəʊl/	....
further education (n)	/ˌfɜːðə(r) edʒuˈkeɪʃn/	....
gadget (n)	/ˈɡædʒɪt/	....
gill (n)	/ɡɪl/	....

WORDLIST

Word	Phonetics	Translation
hen (n)	/hen/	....
herd (n)	/hɜ:d/	....
herd (v)	/hɜ:d/	....
hind leg (n)	/ˌhaɪnd ˈleg/	....
hiss (v)	/hɪs/	....
hoof (n)	/hu:f/	....
horn (n)	/hɔːn/	....
intuitively (adv)	/ɪnˈtjuːɪtɪvli/	....
knuckle (n)	/ˈnʌkl/	....
lamb (n)	/læm/	....
mammal (n)	/ˈmæml/	....
mane (n)	/meɪn/	....
mare (n)	/meə(r)/	....
miaow (v)	/miˈaʊ/	....
pack (n)	/pæk/	....
palm (n)	/pɑːm/	....
paw (n)	/pɔː/	....
piglet (n)	/ˈpɪglət/	....
pile (n)	/paɪl/	....
protect (v)	/prəˈtekt/	....
put (an animal) down (phr v)	/ˌpʊt ˈdaʊn/	....
ram (n)	/ræm/	....
retrieve (v)	/rɪˈtriːv/	....
roar (v)	/rɔː(r)/	....
scales (n)	/skeɪlz/	....
school (n)	/skuːl/	....
scratch (v)	/skrætʃ/	....
shell (n)	/ʃel/	....
smoke (n)	/sməʊk/	....
sow (n)	/saʊ/	....
squawk (v)	/skwɔːk/	....
squeak (v)	/skwiːk/	....
stallion (n)	/ˈstæliən/	....
swarm (n)	/swɔːm/	....
synthesise (v)	/ˈsɪnθəsaɪz/	....
tail (n)	/teɪl/	....
tentacle (n)	/ˈtentəkl/	....
torture (n)	/ˈtɔːtʃə(r)/	....
transmit (n)	/trænsˈmɪt/	....
tusk (n)	/tʌsk/	....
whisker (n)	/ˈwɪskə(r)/	....
whistle (v)	/ˈwɪsl/	....
wing (n)	/wɪŋ/	....
withstand (v)	/wɪðˈstænd/	....

Get ready for your exam 4

Word	Phonetics	Translation
assess (v)	/əˈses/	....
custody (n)	/ˈkʌstədi/	....
legal representation (n)	/ˌliːgl reprɪzenˈteɪʃn/	....
punish (v)	/ˈpʌnɪʃ/	....
sentence (to death) (v)	/ˈsentəns/	....
shelter (v)	/ˈʃeltə(r)/	....
shuttle (v)	/ˈʃʌtl/	....

Unit 5 In the news

Word	Phonetics	Translation
accuse (v)	/əˈkjuːz/	....
advent (the advent of) (n)	/ˈædvent/	....
adventure story (n)	/ədˈventʃə ˌstɔːri/	....
allegedly (adv)	/əˈledʒɪdli/	....
allegory (n)	/ˈæləgəri/	....
appealing (a)	/əˈpiːlɪŋ/	....
axe (v)	/æks/	....
back (v)	/bæk/	....
ban (v)	/bæn/	....
be set (v)	/ˌbi ˈset/	....

Word	Phonetics	Translation
bid (v)	/bɪd/	....
biography (n)	/baɪˈɒgrəfi/	....
blast (n)	/blɑːst/	....
blaze (n)	/bleɪz/	....
boast (v)	/bəʊst/	....
boost (v)	/buːst/	....
breach (v)	/briːtʃ/	....
cash (n)	/kæʃ/	....
clash (v)	/klæʃ/	....
collude (v)	/kəˈluːd/	....
confess (v)	/kənˈfes/	....
cop (n)	/kɒp/	....
counterpart (n)	/ˈkaʊntəpɑːt/	....
crime story (n)	/ˈkraɪm ˌstɔːri/	....
cunning (a)	/ˈkʌnɪŋ/	....
curious (a)	/ˈkjʊəriəs/	....
dart (v)	/dɑːt/	....
dedicated (a)	/ˈdedɪkeɪtɪd/	....
exhilarating (a)	/ɪgˈzɪləreɪtɪŋ/	....
fall (v)	/fɔːl/	....
fantasy (n)	/ˈfæntəsi/	....
fast-moving (a)	/ˌfɑːstˈmuːvɪŋ/	....
fierce (a)	/fɪəs/	....
fine (n)	/faɪn/	....
fluctuate (v)	/ˈflʌktʃueɪt/	....
funny (a)	/ˈfʌni/	....
governing (a)	/ˈgʌvənɪŋ/	....
gripping (a)	/ˈgrɪpɪŋ/	....
historical story (n)	/hɪˈstɒrɪkl ˌstɔːri/	....
hit (v)	/hɪt/	....
horror story (n)	/ˈhɒrə ˌstɔːri/	....
hover (v)	/ˈhɒvə(r)/	....
humorous story (n)	/ˈhjuːmərəs ˌstɔːri/	....
immensely (adv)	/ɪˈmensli/	....
impose (v)	/ɪmˈpəʊz/	....
intricate (a)	/ˈɪntrɪkət/	....
invaded (a)	/ɪnˈveɪdɪd/	....
lash out (phr v)	/ˌlæʃ ˈaʊt/	....
light-hearted (a)	/ˌlaɪtˈhɑːtɪd/	....
loom (v)	/luːm/	....
majority (n)	/məˈdʒɒrəti/	....
make off with (phr v)	/ˌmeɪk ˈɒf wɪð/	....
manipulative (a)	/məˈnɪpjələtɪv/	....
mass-circulation (a)	/ˌmæs sɜːkjəˈleɪʃn/	....
moving (a)	/ˈmuːvɪŋ/	....
mystery (n)	/ˈmɪstri/	....
novel (n)	/ˈnɒvl/	....
obsession (n)	/əbˈseʃn/	....
play (n)	/pleɪ/	....
plea (n)	/pliː/	....
pledge (v)	/pledʒ/	....
plot (n)	/plɒt/	....
poetry (n)	/ˈpəʊətri/	....
pretend (v)	/prɪˈtend/	....
privacy (n)	/ˈprɪvəsi/	....
probe (n)	/prəʊb/	....
provoke (v)	/prəˈvəʊk/	....
publicity (n)	/pʌbˈlɪsəti/	....
pursue (v)	/pəˈsjuː/	....
quit (v)	/kwɪt/	....
relentlessly (adv)	/rɪˈlentləsli/	....
riddle (n)	/ˈrɪdl/	....
rise (v)	/raɪz/	....
romance (n)	/rəʊˈmæns/	....
run (a story) (v)	/rʌn/	....
ruthless (a)	/ˈruːθləs/	....
sack (v)	/sæk/	....
satirical (a)	/səˈtɪrɪkl/	....
scary (a)	/ˈskeəri/	....
science-fiction story (n)	/ˌsaɪənsˈfɪkʃn ˌstɔːri/	....

WORDLIST

Word	Phonetics	Translation
serious (a)	/'sɪəriəs/	....
sharply (adv)	/'ʃɑːpli/	....
short story (n)	/ˌʃɔːt 'stɔːri/	....
soap opera (n)	/'səʊp ˌɒprə/	....
solely (adv)	/'səʊlli/	....
spark (v)	/spɑːk/	....
spring up (phr v)	/ˌsprɪŋ 'ʌp/	....
steadily (adv)	/'stedɪli/	....
sting (v)	/stɪŋ/	....
successive (a)	/sək'sesɪv/	....
surge (n)	/sɜːdʒ/	....
the public eye (in/out of ~) (idiom)	/ðə ˌpʌblɪk 'aɪ/	....
thought-provoking (a)	/'θɔːtprəˌvəʊkɪŋ/	....
top (a)	/tɒp/	....
trace (a call) (v)	/treɪs/	....
twist (in a plot) (n)	/twɪst/	....
wed (v)	/wed/	....

Get ready for your exam 5

Word	Phonetics	Translation
allusion (n)	/ə'luːʒn/	....
bestow (v)	/bɪ'stəʊ/	....
corruption (n)	/kə'rʌpʃn/	....
embodiment (n)	/ɪm'bɒdimənt/	....
endow (v)	/ɪn'daʊ/	....
expose (v)	/ɪk'spəʊz/	....
fundamental (a)	/ˌfʌndə'mentl/	....
indomitable (a)	/ɪn'dɒmɪtəbl/	....
noble (a)	/'nəʊbl/	....
overlook (v)	/ˌəʊvə'lʊk/	....
submission (n)	/səb'mɪʃn/	....

Unit 6 Points of view

Word	Phonetics	Translation
admit (v)	/əd'mɪt/	....
assert (v)	/ə'sɜːt/	....
assume (v)	/ə'sjuːm/	....
at random (idiom)	/ət 'rændəm/	....
audience (n)	/'ɔːdiəns/	....
bear sth in mind (idiom)	/ˌbeə(r) ɪn 'maɪnd/	....
Buddhism (n)	/'bʊdɪzəm/	....
census (n)	/'sensəs/	....
challenger (n)	/'tʃælɪndʒə(r)/	....
Christianity (n)	/ˌkrɪsti'ænəti/	....
church (n)	/tʃɜːtʃ/	....
comment (v)	/'kɒment/	....
connect (with) (v)	/kə'nekt/	....
contestant (n)	/kən'testənt/	....
conventional (a)	/kən'venʃənl/	....
convince (v)	/kən'vɪns/	....
convinced (a)	/kən'vɪnst/	....
crew (n)	/kruː/	....
crucial (a)	/'kruːʃl/	....
deception (n)	/dɪ'sepʃn/	....
decline (v)	/dɪ'klaɪn/	....
deduce (v)	/dɪ'djuːs/	....
deny (v)	/dɪ'naɪ/	....
discrimination (n)	/dɪˌskrɪmɪ'neɪʃn/	....
distressing (a)	/dɪ'stresɪŋ/	....
doubt (have doubts) (n)	/daʊt/	....
doubt (v)	/daʊt/	....
dull (a)	/dʌl/	....
episode (n)	/'epɪsəʊd/	....
fix (results in a show) (v)	/fɪks/	....
frame (of a TV programme) (n)	/freɪm/	....

Word	Phonetics	Translation
go along with sb/sth (phr v)	/ˌgəʊ ə'lɒŋ wɪð/	....
guess (v)	/ges/	....
guilt (n)	/gɪlt/	....
gurdwara (n)	/gɜː'dwɑːrə/	....
head-to-head (a)	/ˌhedtə'hed/	....
Hinduism (n)	/'hɪnduːɪzəm/	....
hoax (n)	/həʊks/	....
identify yourself with sb/sth (phr v)	/aɪ'dentɪfaɪ jɔːˌself wɪð/	....
infer (v)	/ɪn'fɜː(r)/	....
innocent (a)	/'ɪnəsnt/	....
insist (v)	/ɪn'sɪst/	....
Islam (n)	/'ɪzlɑːm/	....
isolation (n)	/ˌaɪsə'leɪʃn/	....
Judaism (n)	/'dʒuːdeɪɪzəm/	....
lawyer (n)	/'lɔːjə(r)/	....
memorise (v)	/'meməraɪz/	....
mosque (n)	/mɒsk/	....
non-violent (a)	/ˌnɒn'vaɪələnt/	....
on air (idiom)	/ˌɒn 'eə(r)/	....
persuade (v)	/pə'sweɪd/	....
producer (n)	/prə'djuːsə(r)/	....
quiz (v)	/kwɪz/	....
ratings (n)	/'reɪtɪŋz/	....
realise (v)	/'riːəlaɪz/	....
reject (v)	/rɪ'dʒekt/	....
self-evidently (adv)	/ˌself'evɪdəntli/	....
Sikhism (n)	/'siːkɪzəm/	....
sponsor (n)	/'spɒnsə(r)/	....
surface (v)	/'sɜːfɪs/	....
suspicious (a)	/sə'spɪʃəs/	....
synagogue (n)	/'sɪnəgɒg/	....
target (n)	/'tɑːgɪt/	....
temple (n)	/'templ/	....
undoubtedly (adv)	/ʌn'daʊtɪdli/	....
vehemently (adv)	/'viːəməntli/	....
wonder (v)	/'wʌndə(r)/	....

Get ready for your exam 6

Word	Phonetics	Translation
alert (v)	/ə'lɜːt/	....
data mining (n)	/'deɪtə ˌmaɪnɪŋ/	....
drawback (n)	/'drɔːbæk/	....
monitor (v)	/'mɒnɪtə(r)/	....
reluctant (a)	/rɪ'lʌktənt/	....
retrieval (n)	/rɪ'triːvl/	....
soar (v)	/sɔː(r)/	....

Unit 7 Putting the world to rights

Word	Phonetics	Translation
access (n)	/'ækses/	....
be to blame (idiom)	/ˌbiː tə 'bleɪm/	....
beckon (v)	/'bekən/	....
bleaching (n)	/'bliːtʃɪŋ/	....
bypass (n)	/'baɪpɑːs/	....
cactus (n)	/'kæktəs/	....
carbon dioxide (n)	/ˌkɑːbən daɪ'ɒksaɪd/	....
carbon emission (n)	/ˌkɑːbən ɪ'mɪʃn/	....
carbon footprint (n)	/ˌkɑːbən 'fʊtprɪnt/	....
charming (a)	/'tʃɑːmɪŋ/	....
climate change (n)	/'klaɪmət ˌtʃeɪndʒ/	....
cloud forest (n)	/'klaʊd ˌfɒrɪst/	....
committed (a)	/kə'mɪtɪd/	....
consumption (n)	/kən'sʌmpʃn/	....
cope (v)	/kəʊp/	....
coral reef (n)	/ˌkɒrəl 'riːf/	....
deal with sth/sb (phr v)	/'diːl wɪð/	....

Word	Phonetics	Translation
decompose (v)	/ˌdiːkəmˈpəʊz/	....
deforestation (n)	/ˌdiːˌfɒrɪˈsteɪʃn/	....
destructive (a)	/dɪˈstrʌktɪv/	....
developing country (n)	/dɪˈveləpɪŋ ˌkʌntri/	....
dairy-free (a)	/ˌdeəriˈfriː/	....
digger (n)	/ˈdɪgə(r)/	....
dire (a)	/ˈdaɪə(r)/	....
disgust (n)	/dɪsˈgʌst/	....
drought (n)	/draʊt/	....
economic growth (n)	/ˌiːkəˌnɒmɪk ˈgrəʊθ/	....
endangered species (n)	/ɪnˌdeɪndʒəd ˈspiːʃiːz/	....
energy-saving (a)	/ˈenədʒiˌseɪvɪŋ/	....
extinct (a)	/ɪkˈstɪŋkt/	....
fauna (n)	/ˈfɔːnə/	....
fertiliser (n)	/ˈfɜːtəlaɪzə(r)/	....
flora (n)	/ˈflɔːrə/	....
fossil fuel (n)	/ˈfɒsl ˌfjuːəl/	....
global warming (n)	/ˌgləʊbl ˈwɔːmɪŋ/	....
greedy (a)	/ˈgriːdi/	....
greenhouse effect (n)	/ˈgriːnhaʊs ɪˌfekt/	....
greenhouse gases (n)	/ˌgriːnhaʊs ˈgæsɪz/	....
halal (n)	/ˈhælæl/	....
heat wave (n)	/ˈhiːtweɪv/	....
heavy goods vehicle (n)	/ˌhevi ˈgʊdz ˌviːəkl/	....
high-fibre (a)	/ˌhaɪˈfaɪbə(r)/	....
hybrid (a)	/ˈhaɪbrɪd/	....
ice cap (n)	/ˈaɪs kæp/	....
impressed (a)	/ɪmˈprest/	....
industrialised country (n)	/ɪnˈdʌstriəlaɪzd ˌkʌntri/	....
interest group (n)	/ˈɪntrest ˌgruːp/	....
ivy (n)	/ˈaɪvi/	....
kiss goodbye to sth (idiom)	/ˌkɪs gʊdˈbaɪ tə/	....
kosher (a)	/ˈkəʊʃə(r)/	....
landfill site (n)	/ˈlændfɪl ˌsaɪt/	....
low-calorie (a)	/ˌləʊˈkæləri/	....
low-carb (a)	/ˌləʊˈkɑːb/	....
low-sodium (a)	/ˌləʊˈsəʊdiəm/	....
lumber (v)	/ˈlʌmbə(r)/	....
melt (v)	/melt/	....
methane (n)	/ˈmiːθeɪn/	....
monument (n)	/ˈmɒnjəmənt/	....
natural habitat (n)	/ˌnætrəl ˈhæbɪtæt/	....
nuclear power (n)	/ˌnjuːkliə ˈpaʊə(r)/	....
oak (n)	/əʊk/	....
on standby (a)	/ɒn ˈstændbaɪ/	....
orchid (n)	/ˈɔːkɪd/	....
organic (a)	/ɔːˈgænɪk/	....
packaging (n)	/ˈpækədʒɪŋ/	....
palm (n)	/pɑːm/	....
pine (n)	/paɪn/	....
polyp (n)	/ˈpɒlɪp/	....
poppy (n)	/ˈpɒpi/	....
primeval forest (n)	/praɪˌmiːvl ˈfɒrɪst/	....
public outcry (n)	/ˌpʌblɪk ˈaʊtkraɪ/	....
pump sth out (phr v)	/ˌpʌmp ˈaʊt/	....
recyclable (a)	/ˌriːˈsaɪkləbl/	....
redistribution (n)	/ˌriːdɪstrɪˈbjuːʃn/	....
renewable energy (n)	/rɪˌnjuːəbl ˈenədʒi/	....
rev up (phr v)	/ˌrev ˈʌp/	....
rose (n)	/rəʊz/	....
run-off (n)	/ˈrʌnɒf/	....
sea level (n)	/ˈsiː levl/	....
secure (v)	/sɪˈkjʊə(r)/	....
sell-by date (n)	/ˈselbaɪ ˌdeɪt/	....
solar panel (n)	/ˌsəʊlə ˈpænl/	....
solar power (n)	/ˌsəʊlə ˈpaʊə(r)/	....
specialise (v)	/ˈspeʃəlaɪz/	....
struggle (n)	/ˈstrʌgl/	....
sunflower (n)	/ˈsʌnflaʊə(r)/	....

Word	Phonetics	Translation
supply (n)	/səˈplaɪ/	....
swathe (n)	/sweɪð/	....
thermostat (n)	/ˈθɜːməstæt/	....
threat (n)	/θret/	....
thrive on (phr v)	/ˈθraɪv ɒn/	....
trap (v)	/træp/	....
trigger (v)	/ˈtrɪgə(r)/	....
tumble dryer (n)	/ˌtʌmbl ˈdraɪə(r)/	....
turbine (n)	/ˈtɜːbaɪn/	....
urgent (a)	/ˈɜːdʒənt/	....
vegan (n) (a)	/ˈviːgən/	....
vegetarian (n) (a)	/ˌvedʒəˈteəriən/	....
vulnerable (a)	/ˈvʌlnərəbl/	....
waste (v)	/weɪst/	....
whole-grain (a)	/ˈhəʊlgreɪn/	....

Get ready for your exam 7

Word	Phonetics	Translation
barbarian (n)	/bɑːˈbeəriən/	....
civilised (a)	/ˈsɪvəlaɪzd/	....
contradict (v)	/ˌkɒntrəˈdɪkt/	....
cultivated (a)	/ˈkʌltɪveɪtɪd/	....
dominate (v)	/ˈdɒmɪneɪt/	....
elaborate (a)	/ɪˈlæbərət/	....
exhaustive (a)	/ɪgˈzɔːstɪv/	....
intervention (n)	/ˌɪntəˈvenʃn/	....
invariably (adv)	/ɪnˈveəriəbli/	....
lengthy (a)	/ˈleŋθi/	....
notion (n)	/ˈnəʊʃn/	....
obesity (n)	/əʊˈbiːsəti/	....
regulated (a)	/ˈregjəleɪtɪd/	....
toxin (n)	/ˈtɒksɪn/	....
trace (n)	/treɪs/	....
wild (a)	/waɪld/	....
wreck (v)	/rek/	....

Unit 8 Caught in the net

Word	Phonetics	Translation
address bar (n)	/əˈdres ˌbɑː(r)/	....
application (n)	/ˌæplɪˈkeɪʃn/	....
back button (n)	/ˈbæk ˌbʌtn/	....
bid (n)	/bɪd/	....
broadband (n)	/ˈbrɔːdbænd/	....
call sth off (phr v)	/ˌkɔːl ˈɒf/	....
carry on (phr v)	/ˌkæri ˈɒn/	....
command (n)	/kəˈmɑːnd/	....
compulsion (n)	/kəmˈpʌlʃn/	....
conflict (v)	/kənˈflɪkt/	....
conflict (n)	/ˈkɒnflɪkt/	....
decrease (v)	/dɪˈkriːs/	....
decrease (n)	/ˈdiːkriːs/	....
desktop (n)	/ˈdesktɒp/	....
document (n)	/ˈdɒkjəmənt/	....
drag (v)	/dræg/	....
entrepreneur (n)	/ˌɒntrəprəˈnɜː (r)/	....
envy (v)	/ˈenvi/	....
export (v)	/ɪkˈspɔːt/	....
export (n)	/ˈekspɔːt/	....
faulty (a)	/ˈfɔːlti/	....
gender (n)	/ˈdʒendə(r)/	....
generation (n)	/ˌdʒenəˈreɪʃn/	....
hack (v)	/hæk/	....
hard drive (n)	/ˈhɑːd ˌdraɪv/	....
have sb on (phr v)	/ˌhæv ˈɒn/	....
icon (n)	/ˈaɪkɒn/	....
inundate (v)	/ˈɪnʌndeɪt/	....
legacy (n)	/ˈlegəsi/	....
log off (phr v)	/ˌlɒg ˈɒf/	....

WORDLIST

Word	Phonetics	Translation
log on (phr v)	/ˌlɒg ˈɒn/	
menu (n)	/ˈmenjuː/	
milestone (n)	/ˈmaɪlstəʊn/	
minimise (v)	/ˈmɪnɪmaɪz/	
non-profit (a)	/ˌnɒnˈprɒfɪt/	
opt out of sth (phr v)	/ˌɒpt ˈaʊt/	
outcry (n)	/ˈaʊtkraɪ/	
parental lock (n)	/pəˌrentl ˈlɒk/	
pass sth on (phr v)	/ˌpɑːs ˈɒn/	
permit (v)	/pəˈmɪt/	
permit (n)	/ˈpɜːmɪt/	
petition (n)	/pəˈtɪʃn/	
produce (v)	/prəˈdjuːs/	
produce (n)	/ˈprɒdjuːs/	
profile (n)	/ˈprəʊfaɪl/	
protest (v)	/prəˈtest/	
protest (n)	/ˈprəʊtest/	
put sb off (phr v)	/ˌpʊt ˈɒf/	
record (v)	/rɪˈkɔːd/	
record (n)	/ˈrekɔːd/	
reference (n)	/ˈrefrəns/	
refund (v)	/rɪˈfʌnd/	
refund (n)	/ˈriːfʌnd/	
reputation (n)	/ˌrepjuˈteɪʃn/	
save (v)	/seɪv/	
scroll (n)	/skrəʊl/	
sector (n)	/ˈsektə(r)/	
set off (phr v)	/ˌset ˈɒf/	
show off (phr v)	/ˌʃəʊ ˈɒf/	
skill (n)	/skɪl/	
software (n)	/ˈsɒftweə(r)/	
suspect (v)	/səˈspekt/	
suspect (n)	/ˈsʌspekt/	
swiftly (adv)	/ˈswɪftli/	
take sth on (phr v)	/ˌteɪk ˈɒn/	
three-dimensional (a)	/ˌθriːdaɪˈmenʃənl/	
thumbnail (n)	/ˈθʌmneɪl/	
trace (v)	/treɪs/	
transport (v)	/trænˈspɔːt/	
transport (n)	/ˈtrænspɔːt/	
virtual (a)	/ˈvɜːtʃuəl/	
virus (n)	/ˈvaɪrəs/	
web browser (n)	/ˈweb ˌbraʊzə(r)/	
wireless network (n)	/ˈwaɪələs ˌnetwɜːk/	

Get ready for your exam 8

Word	Phonetics	Translation
acquaintance (n)	/əˈkweɪntəns/	
bare your soul (to sb) (idiom)	/ˌbeə jɔː ˈsəʊl/	
gossip (v)	/ˈgɒsɪp/	
innermost (a)	/ˈɪnəməʊst/	
Internet service provider (n)	/ˌɪntənet ˈsɜːvɪs prəˌvaɪdə(r)/	
repercussion (n)	/ˌriːpəˈkʌʃn/	

Unit 9 A step on the ladder

Word	Phonetics	Translation
academic (a)	/ˌækəˈdemɪk/	
arduous (a)	/ˈɑːdjuəs/	
background (n)	/ˈbækgraʊnd/	
barrister (n)	/ˈbærɪstə(r)/	
bricklayer (n)	/ˈbrɪkleɪə(r)/	
call off (phr v)	/ˌkɔːl ˈɒf/	
chant (v)	/tʃɑːnt/	
come along (phr v)	/ˌkʌm əˈlɒŋ/	
compulsory (a)	/kəmˈpʌlsəri/	

Word	Phonetics	Translation
construction (n)	/kənˈstrʌkʃn/	
core (a)	/kɔː(r)/	
crush (v)	/krʌʃ/	
dedicated to (a)	/ˈdedɪkeɪtɪd ˌtə/	
degree (n)	/dɪˈgriː/	
dilemma (n)	/dɪˈlemə/	
director of studies (n)	/dəˌrektə(r) əv ˈstʌdiz/	
end your days (idiom)	/ˌend jɔː ˈdeɪz/	
fade away (phr v)	/ˌfeɪd əˈweɪ/	
flexible (a)	/ˈfleksəbl/	
further education (n)	/ˌfɜːðə(r) edʒuˈkeɪʃn/	
gaze (v)	/geɪz/	
graduate (n)	/ˈgrædʒuət/	
higher education (n)	/ˌhaɪə(r) edʒuˈkeɪʃn/	
influx (n)	/ˈɪnflʌks/	
joiner (n)	/ˈdʒɔɪnə(r)/	
lecturer (n)	/ˈlektʃərə(r)/	
massive (a)	/ˈmæsɪv/	
maternity leave (n)	/məˈtɜːnəti ˌliːv/	
melting pot (n)	/ˈmeltɪŋ ˌpɒt/	
minimum wage (n)	/ˌmɪnɪməm ˈweɪdʒ/	
motivate (v)	/ˈməʊtɪveɪt/	
nine to five (idiom)	/ˌnaɪn tə ˈfaɪv/	
notice (n)	/ˈnəʊtɪs/	
nurse (n)	/nɜːs/	
overtime (n)	/ˈəʊvətaɪm/	
pass sb by (phr v)	/ˌpɑːs ˈbaɪ/	
poverty (n)	/ˈpɒvəti/	
predominantly (adv)	/prɪˈdɒmɪnəntli/	
promote (v)	/prəˈməʊt/	
reception class (n)	/rɪˈsepʃn ˌklɑːs/	
redundant (a)	/rɪˈdʌndənt/	
repeat (a year in school) (v)	/rɪˈpiːt/	
reputation (n)	/ˌrepjuˈteɪʃn/	
resent (v)	/rɪˈzent/	
resign (v)	/rɪˈzaɪn/	
retail (a)	/ˈriːteɪl/	
(get) the sack (n)	/ˈget ðə ˈsæk/	
sales assistant (n)	/ˈseɪlz əˌsɪstənt/	
scholar (n)	/ˈskɒlə(r)/	
shatter (v)	/ˈʃætə(r)/	
shift work (n)	/ˈʃɪftwɜːk/	
software developer (n)	/ˈsɒftweə dɪˌveləpə(r)/	
solicitor (n)	/səˈlɪsɪtə(r)/	
store manager (n)	/ˈstɔː ˌmænɪdʒə(r)/	
surgeon (n)	/ˈsɜːdʒən/	
undergraduate (n)	/ˌʌndəˈgrædʒuət/	
unemployed (a)	/ˌʌnɪmˈplɔɪd/	
vocational (a)	/vəˈkeɪʃənl/	
web designer (n)	/ˈweb dɪˌzaɪnə(r)/	
well-presented (a)	/ˌwel prɪˈzentɪd/	

Get ready for your exam 9

Word	Phonetics	Translation
angst-ridden (a)	/ˈæŋst ˌrɪdn/	
destitute (a)	/ˈdestɪtjuːt/	
diplomatic (a)	/ˌdɪpləˈmætɪk/	
disguise (v)	/dɪsˈgaɪz/	
euphemism (n)	/ˈjuːfəmɪzəm/	
grubby (a)	/ˈgrʌbi/	
indicator (n)	/ˈɪndɪkeɪtə(r)/	
irrelevance (n)	/ɪˈreləvəns/	
menial (a)	/ˈmiːniəl/	
posh (a)	/pɒʃ/	
privileged (a)	/ˈprɪvəlɪdʒd/	
reliance (n)	/rɪˈlaɪəns/	

WORDLIST

Word	Phonetics	Translation

Unit 10 Out of this world

Word	Phonetics	Translation
altitude (n)	/ˈæltɪtjuːd/	....
asteroid (n)	/ˈæstərɔɪd/	....
astronaut (n)	/ˈæstrənɔːt/	....
astronomer (n)	/əˈstrɒnəmə(r)/	....
atmosphere (n)	/ˈætməsfɪə(r)/	....
banter (v)	/ˈbæntə(r)/	....
booster (n)	/ˈbuːstə(r)/	....
capsule (n)	/ˈkæpsjuːl/	....
capture (v)	/ˈkæptʃə(r)/	....
check over (phr v)	/ˌtʃek ˈəʊvə(r)/	....
comet (n)	/ˈkɒmɪt/	....
confession (n)	/kənˈfeʃn/	....
constellation (n)	/ˌkɒnstəˈleɪʃn/	....
contract (v)	/kənˈtrækt/	....
controversial (a)	/ˌkɒntrəˈvɜːʃl/	....
cope (v)	/kəʊp/	....
cosmos (n)	/ˈkɒzmɒs/	....
crash-land (v)	/ˌkræʃˈlænd/	....
crater (n)	/ˈkreɪtə(r)/	....
creep up (phr v)	/ˌkriːp ˈʌp/	....
crew (n)	/kruː/	....
disappear (v)	/ˌdɪsəˈpɪə(r)/	....
dress rehearsal (n)	/ˌdres rɪˈhɜːsl/	....
flee (v)	/fliː/	....
flying saucer (n)	/ˌflaɪɪŋ ˈsɔːsə(r)/	....
galaxy (n)	/ˈgæləksi/	....
get at (phr v)	/ˈget ət/	....
get away (phr v)	/ˌget əˈweɪ/	....
get back (phr v)	/ˌget ˈbæk/	....
get behind (phr v)	/ˌget bɪˈhaɪnd/	....
get by (phr v)	/ˌget ˈbaɪ/	....
go through (phr v)	/ˌgəʊ ˈθruː/	....
gravity (n)	/ˈgrævəti/	....
hatch (n)	/hætʃ/	....
head out (phr v)	/ˌhed ˈaʊt/	....
heresy (n)	/ˈherəsi/	....
ignite (v)	/ɪgˈnaɪt/	....
instinctively (adv)	/ɪnˈstɪŋktɪvli/	....
intact (a)	/ɪnˈtækt/	....
keep out (phr v)	/ˌkiːp ˈaʊt/	....
launch (v)	/lɔːntʃ/	....
lever (n)	/ˈliːvə(r)/	....
man-made (a)	/ˌmænˈmeɪd/	....
manoeuvre (n)	/məˈnuːvə(r)/	....
manuscript (n)	/ˈmænjuskrɪpt/	....
meteor (n)	/ˈmiːtiɔː(r)/	....
mission control (n)	/ˌmɪʃn kənˈtrəʊl/	....
mission (n)	/ˈmɪʃn/	....
orbit (v) & (n)	/ˈɔːbɪt/	....
planet (n)	/ˈplænɪt/	....
put on (phr v)	/ˌpʊt ˈɒn/	....
ray gun (n)	/ˈreɪ ˌgʌn/	....
re-enter (v)	/ˌriːˈentə(r)/	....
risky (a)	/ˈrɪski/	....
rotate (v)	/rəʊˈteɪt/	....
ruins (n)	/ˈruːɪnz/	....
satellite (n)	/ˈsætəlaɪt/	....
scepticism (n)	/ˈskeptɪsɪzəm/	....
simulator (n)	/ˈsɪmjəleɪtə(r)/	....
slow down (phr v)	/ˌsləʊ ˈdaʊn/	....
solar system (n)	/ˈsəʊlə ˌsɪstəm/	....
space shuttle (n)	/ˈspeɪs ˌʃʌtl/	....
space station (n)	/ˈspeɪs ˌsteɪʃn/	....
spacecraft (n)	/ˈspeɪskrɑːft/	....
start up (phr v)	/ˌstɑːt ˈʌp/	....
supernova (n)	/ˌsuːpəˈnəʊvə/	....
take in (phr v)	/ˌteɪk ˈɪn/	....
the naked eye (idiom)	/ðə ˌneɪkɪd ˈaɪ/	....

Word	Phonetics	Translation
tombstone (n)	/ˈtuːmstəʊn/	....
touch down (v)	/ˌtʌtʃ ˈdaʊn/	....
vanish (v)	/ˈvænɪʃ/	....
velocity gauge (n)	/vəˈlɒsəti ˌgeɪdʒ/	....
vibration (n)	/vaɪˈbreɪʃn/	....

Get ready for your exam 10

Word	Phonetics	Translation
engage in (phr v)	/ɪnˈgeɪdʒ ɪn/	....
hibernate (v)	/ˈhaɪbəneɪt/	....
realism (n)	/ˈrɪəlɪzm/	....
regain (v)	/rɪˈgeɪn/	....
spacecraft (n)	/ˈspeɪskrɑːft/	....

OXFORD
UNIVERSITY PRESS

Great Clarendon Street, Oxford OX2 6DP

Oxford University Press is a department of the University of Oxford.
It furthers the University's objective of excellence in research, scholarship,
and education by publishing worldwide in

Oxford New York

Auckland Cape Town Dar es Salaam Hong Kong Karachi
Kuala Lumpur Madrid Melbourne Mexico City Nairobi
New Delhi Shanghai Taipei Toronto

With offices in

Argentina Austria Brazil Chile Czech Republic France Greece
Guatemala Hungary Italy Japan Poland Portugal Singapore
South Korea Switzerland Thailand Turkey Ukraine Vietnam

OXFORD and OXFORD ENGLISH are registered trade marks of
Oxford University Press in the UK and in certain other countries

ACKNOWLEDGEMENTS

*The publisher and authors are grateful to the many teachers and students who read
and piloted the manuscript, and provided invaluable feedback. With special thanks to
the following for their contribution to the development of the Solutions series:*
Zinta Andzane, Latvia; Irena Budreikiene, Lithuania; Kati Elekes, Hungary;
Danica Gondová, Slovakia; Ferenc Kelemen, Hungary; Natasha Koltko,
Ukraine; Mario Maleta, Croatia; Juraj Marcek, Slovakia; Dace Miška, Latvia;
Anna Morris, Ukraine; Hana Musílková, Czech Republic; Zsuzsanna Nyirő,
Hungary; Eva Paulerová, Czech Republic; Hana Pavliková, Czech Republic;
Zoltán Rézműves, Hungary; Rita Rudiatiene, Lithuania; Dagmar Škorpíková,
Czech Republic

*The authors and publishers are grateful to those who have given permission to
reproduce the following extracts and adaptations of copyright material:*
p19 extract from 'Want to know detail about the advantages and
disadvantages of money?' from *Yahoo! Answers.* Reproduced with permission
of Yahoo! Inc. ® 2008 by Yahoo! Inc. YAHOO! And the YAHOO! Logo are
trademarks of Yahoo! Inc.
p19 extract adapted from ODYSSEY's website at www.odysseymagazine.com
© 2008, Carus Publishing Company, published by Cobblestone Publishing,
30 Grove Street, Suite C, Peterborough, NH 03458. All Rights Reserved. Used
by permission of the publisher.
p25 'Make Space Youth Review' © 4Children 2007, summary of Youth
Review findings available at www.makespace.org.uk. Reproduced by
permission of 4Children.

p59 'What's green and flies? An eco-hypocrite who won't stay grounded,
say researchers' by David Derbyshire, 30 August 2007 from The Daily Mail.
Reproduced by permission of The Daily Mail.
p61 'War on waste as families each bin food worth £370' by Lindsay McIntosh,
2 November 2007, from The Scotsman. Reproduced by permission of The
Scotsman.
p73 extract adapted from 'A Not-So-Itsy-Bitsy Web' by Vickie An, 31 August
2007, from www.timeforkids.com. © 2007 Time For Kids and Time Inc. All
rights reserved. Reproduced by permission.
p92 extract adapted from 'The Secret Language of Dolphins' by Crispin Boyer
from www.kids.nationalgeographic.com. © National Geographic. Reproduced
by permission.
p93 extract adapted from 'Jakubisko film puts Báthory legend in a different
light', by Stefan M. Hogan, 3 September 2007, from *The Slovak Spectator.*
Reproduced by permission.
p93 extract adapted from 'UCLA/VA Research Analysis in Journal Nature
Explains Wide Variations in Animal Sleep Habits' by Dan Pagel, 26 October
2005, from www.newsroom.ucla.edu. Reproduced by permission of the
University of California, Los Angeles.
p94 extract adapted from an interview with Pamela Lippe from
www.timeforkids.com © 2007 Time For Kids and Time Inc. All rights reserved.
Reproduced by permission.
p95 transcript from The Lab, 'No Bag Thanks' by Karen Pearce, first published
in 2003, is reproduced by permission of the Australian Broadcasting
Corporation and ABC Online © 2003 ABC. All rights reserved.
p98 adapted from 'Dead dog's owner creates FIVE cloned puppies of her
beloved pet' by Fiona Macrae, 5 August 2008, *Daily Mail Online.* Reproduced by
permission of Solo Syndication.
p99 adapted from 'World's Oldest Newspaper Goes Digital', 5 February 2007,
from www.editorandpublisher.com. Used with permission of Nielsen Business
Media, Inc.

Although every effort has been made to trace and contact copyright holders
before publication, this has not been possible in some cases. We apologize for
any apparent infringement of copyright and if notified, the publisher will be
pleased to rectify any errors or omissions at the earliest opportunity.

Illustration commissioning and picture research by: Helen Reilly/Arnos
Design Ltd

Illustrations by: Arnos Design Ltd p29; Andy Parker pp32, 57, 90; Martin Shovel
pp22, 26, 44, 66, 70, 71, 76.

*The publisher would like to thank the following for their permission to reproduce
photographs:* Alamy pp9 (class outside), 13 (Israel images), 25 (Photofusion
Picture Library), 27 (Jim West), 31 (fox hunting); 88 (alien/L. Zacharie), 63
(compost/bikes/wind turbine/wood burner/wheelie bin), 64, 74 (volunteer/man
in car/people on bus), 75 (miner and nurse), 94 (Covent Garden/Thai market/
European city), 96 (man painting), 100 (Florida campsite); Arnos Design Ltd
pp59, 67; Bubbles p52 (mother and son); Corbis pp10 (Eliane/Zefa), 28 (three
teen girls/three teen boys/Grove Pashley), 34 (Polar bear/Image Source) 40
(teenagers/Rainer Elstermann/zefa), 48 (Bettman), 53 (Simon Jarrat), 75 (farmer/
Jim Craigmyle), 77 (beach/John Carnemolla), 80, 85 (Douglas Kirkland); Fotolia
pp49, 97, 99; Getty Images/Superstudio pp20 (swimming champion), 23
(AFP), 39 (Christmas shoppers/Stephen Chemin), 40 (police), 41 (Time&Life
Pictures), 43 (Margaret Bourke-White/Time&Life Pictures) (bread line/Margaret
Bourke-White/Time&Life Pictures), 46, 79 (Uma Thurman/Film Magic);
Istockphoto pp12 (webking), 20 (graduation), 30 (Hedda Gjerpen), 35 (mice), 36
(Everglades), 63 (solar panel); 101 (Jim Jurica); OUP p9 (class/students/nursery);
PA Photos pp69 (Eckehard Schulz/AP), 79 (Bill Gates/Orban Thierry/ABACA);
Photolibrary p61 (both); Punchstock pp75 (Digital Vision), 81 (Blend), 98; Rex
Features pp8 (both), 15, 62, 79 (Russell Simmons), 87; The Kobal Collection p7
(20thCenturyFox/Paramount); The Science Photo Library pp84 (Venus/Chris
Bjornberg), (Beagle/European Space Agency), 89 (David A. Hardy).

Although every effort has been made to trace and contact copyright holders
before publication, this has not been possible in some cases. We apologize for
any apparent infringement of copyright and if notified, the publisher will be
pleased to rectify any errors or omissions at the earliest opportunity.

Answer for 9B exercise 2: Alex was too short to reach the button for the
12th floor.